LEADER'S GUIDE

Dr. Kathleen A. Farmer, the writer of this study book, is Professor of Old Testament at United Theological Seminary, Dayton, Ohio, where she has taught since receiving her Ph.D. from Southern Methodist University in 1978. Dr. Farmer is a lay member of Fairview United Methodist Church in Dayton. She frequently teaches in adult church school classes in the Dayton area. Her recent publications include *Proverbs and Ecclesiastes: Who Knows What Is Good?* (Eerdmans, 1991) and "Psalms" in *The Women's Bible Commentary*, Carol A. Newsome and Sharon H. Ringe, editors (Westminster/John Knox Press, 1992). Dr. Farmer is also the writer of Volume 3 of JOURNEY THROUGH THE BIBLE: JOSHUA, JUDGES, RUTH.

JOB, PSALMS, PROVERBS, ECCLESIASTES, SONG OF SOLOMON

Copyright © 1995 by Cokesbury
All rights reserved.

JOURNEY THROUGH THE BIBLE: JOB, PSALMS, PROVERBS, ECCLESIASTES, SONG OF SOLOMON, LEADER'S GUIDE. An official resource for The United Methodist Church prepared by the General Board of Discipleship through the Division of Church School Publications and published by Cokesbury, The United Methodist Publishing House; 201 Eighth Avenue, South; P. O. Box 801; Nashville, Tennessee 37202-0801. Printed in the United States of America.

Scripture quotations in this publication, unless otherwise indicated, are from the New Revised Standard Version of the Bible, copyrighted © 1989 by the Division of Christian Education of the National Council of the Churches of Christ in the United States of America, and are used by permission. All rights reserved.

For permission to reproduce any material in this publication, call 615-749-6421, or write to Permissions Office; 201 Eighth Avenue, South; P. O. Box 801, Nashville, Tennessee 37202-0801.

To orders copies of this publication, call toll free: 800-672-1789. Call Monday through Friday, 7:00–6:30 Central Time; 5:00–4:30 Pacific Time; Saturday, 9:00–5:00. You may FAX your order to 800-445-8189. Telecommunication Device for the Deaf/Telex Telephone: 800-227-4091. Automated order system is available after office hours. Use your Cokesbury account, American Express, Visa, Discover, or MasterCard.

EDITORIAL TEAM

Mary Leslie Dawson-Ramsey,
Editor

Norma L. Bates,
Assistant Editor

Linda O. Spicer,
Adult Section Assistant

DESIGN TEAM

Ed Wynne,
Layout Designer

Susan J. Scruggs,
Design Supervisor,
Cover Design

ADMINISTRATIVE STAFF

Neil M. Alexander,
Vice-President, Publishing

Duane A. Ewers,
Editor of Church School Publications

Gary L. Ball-Kilbourne,
Senior Editor, Adult Publications

 Cokesbury

04– 10 9 8 7 6 5 4

THIS PUBLICATION IS PRINTED ON RECYCLED PAPER

CONTENTS

Volume 6: Job—Song of Solomon   by Kathleen A. Farmer

INTRODUCTION TO THE SERIES		2
Chapter 1	THE "PATIENCE" OF JOB?	3
Chapter 2	"WITH FRIENDS LIKE THESE..."	8
Chapter 3	"WHERE WERE YOU WHEN I LAID THE FOUNDATION OF THE EARTH?"	13
Chapter 4	SEASONS OF THE HEART AND SPIRIT	18
Chapter 5	"WHOM HAVE I IN HEAVEN BUT YOU?"	23
Chapter 6	WITH THE LORD THERE IS STEADFAST LOVE	28
Chapter 7	"MY GOD, MY GOD, WHY HAVE YOU FORSAKEN ME?"	33
Chapter 8	"WISDOM CRIES OUT IN THE STREET"	38
Chapter 9	"WISDOM IS A FOUNTAIN OF LIFE"	43
Chapter 10	"THE EYES OF THE LORD KEEP WATCH OVER KNOWLEDGE"	48
Chapter 11	VANITY OF VANITIES	53
Chapter 12	THE POWER OF POSITIVE PESSIMISM	58
Chapter 13	"MANY WATERS CANNOT QUENCH LOVE"	63
A CLOSER LOOK AT THE PSALMS		68
POPULAR THEOLOGY IN WISDOM LITERATURE AND PSALMS		70
PROVERBS: SAMPLING THE SHORTER SAYINGS		71
SAMPLE PSALM-LINE		Inside back cover

Introduction to the Series

The leader's guides provided for use with JOURNEY THROUGH THE BIBLE make the following assumptions:
- adults learn in different ways:
  - —by reading
  - —by listening to speakers
  - —by working on projects
  - —by drama and roleplay
  - —by using their imaginations
  - —by expressing themselves creatively
  - —by teaching others
- the mix of persons in your group is different from that found in any other group;
- the length of the actual time you have for teaching in a session may vary from thirty minutes to ninety minutes;
- the physical place where your class meets is not exactly like the place where any other group or class meets;
- your teaching skills, experiences, and preferences are unlike anyone else's.

We encourage you to discover and develop the ways you can best use the information and learning ideas in this leader's guide with your particular class. To get started, we suggest you try following these steps:

1. Think and pray about your individual class members. Who are they? What are they like? Why are they involved in this particular Bible study class at this particular time in their lives? What seem to be their needs? How do you think they learn best?
2. Think and pray about your class members as a group. A group takes on a character that can be different from the particular characters of the individuals who make up that group. How do your class members interact? What do they enjoy doing together? What would help them become stronger as a group?
3. Keep in mind that you are teaching this class for the sake of the class members, in order to help them increase in their faithfulness as disciples of Jesus Christ. Teachers sometimes fall prey to the danger of teaching in ways that are easiest for themselves. The best teachers accept the discomfort of taking risks and stretching their teaching skills in order to focus on what will really help the class members learn and grow in their faith.
4. Read the chapter in the study book. Read the assigned Bible passages. Read the background Bible passages, if any. Work through the Dimension 1 questions in the study book. Make a list of any items you do not understand and need to research further using such tools as Bible dictionaries, concordances, Bible atlases, and commentaries. In other words, do your homework. Be prepared with your own knowledge about the Bible passages being studied by your class.
5. Read the chapter's material in the leader's guide. You might want to begin with the "Additional Bible Helps," found at the *end* of each chapter in the leader's guide. Then look at each learning idea in the "Learning Menu."
6. Spend some time with the "Learning Menu." Notice that the "Learning Menu" is organized around Dimensions 1, 2, and 3 in the study book. Recognizing that different adults and adult classes will learn best using different teaching/learning methods, in each of the three dimensions you will find
   - —at least one learning idea that is primarily discussion based;
   - —at least one learning idea that begins with a method other than discussion, but which may lead into discussion.

   Make notes about which learning ideas will work best given the unique makeup and setting of your class.
7. Decide on a lesson plan: Which learning ideas will you lead the class members through when? What materials will you need? What other preparations do you need to make? How long do you plan to spend on a particular learning idea?
8. Many experienced teachers have found that they do better if they plan more than they actually use during a class session. They also know that their class members may become frustrated if they try to do too much during a class session. In other words
   - —plan more than you can actually use. That way, you have back-up learning ideas in case something does not work well or something takes much less time than you thought.
   - —don't try to do everything listed in the "Learning Menu." We have intentionally offered you much more than you can use in one class session.
   - —be flexible while you teach. A good lesson plan is only a guide for your use as you teach people. Keep the focus on your class members, not your lesson plan.
9. After you teach, evaluate the class session. What worked well? What did not? What did you learn from your experience of teaching that will help you plan for the next class session?

May God's Spirit be upon you as you lead your class on their *Journey Through the Bible*!

Questions or comments? Call Curric-U-Phone 1-800-251-8591.

1
The "Patience" of Job?

Job 1–3; 42:7-9

Introduction to this Volume
As you begin this volume in JOURNEY THROUGH THE BIBLE, you may want to spend a few minutes looking over the materials that will be covered in the weeks ahead. Look at the Table of Contents found in the front of most Bibles. Note that in most Christian Bibles the books of Job, Psalms, Proverbs, Ecclesiastes, and The Song of Solomon are found sandwiched in between the "historical" books and the Prophets. Christian Bibles arrange the books in the same order as did the early Greek translation (known as the Septuagint [SEP-too-uh-jint]).

The books studied in volumes 1–5 of JOURNEY THROUGH THE BIBLE were all concerned with some part of the history of the people of Israel. But the books to be studied in this volume (with the exception of a few Psalms) seldom mention Israel's history.

The books of Genesis through Esther are mostly written in prose and contain few poetic passages. The books of Job, Psalms, Proverbs, Ecclesiastes, and The Song of Solomon are written mostly in poetry and contain only a few prose passages.

The very nature of poetic language makes these books both more appealing to the modern reader *and* more difficult for the modern reader to understand. Poetry often speaks of human nature and human experiences with which modern readers themselves can easily identify.

On the other hand, poetry contains what one scholar has called "densely patterned meaning." The author or speaker deliberately packs as many meanings as possible into the words of a poetic text. This complicates the task of interpretation to an enormous degree.

LEARNING MENU

Dimension One activities are designed to help you and class members develop a habit of checking what the biblical text actually says.

Dimension Two options should help you and your class members consider what the text meant in its original setting. You and your students should have opportunities to exercise both your imaginations and your critical thinking abilities. How was a phrase or an action or a gesture understood in its own culture? How did a story or a report function in its earliest contexts?

Dimension Three options ask you and your class members to personalize your learnings in order to let the biblical texts speak in your lives. How can these texts influence your faith or your culture? What questions do these texts raise about the way you think and act as a person of faith in today's world? How might the people of God respond to these texts from the midst of their own life-settings?

For each of the three Dimensions two or more options are provided from which you are invited to choose at least one option. Choices should reflect what you think about the learning styles, experiences, and interests of your class members.

Dimension 1: What Does the Bible Say?

(A) Hold an opening worship time.

- Begin your class time together with a brief worship time. Offer a few moments of silence. Conclude with the reading of Psalm 121.

(B) Discuss Dimension 1 questions from the study book.

- The preferred method for working on Dimension 1 is to ask participants to complete the questions in advance of the class session. Then you may spend a short amount of time sharing and discussing ideas. The intent of Dimension 1 is to provide a quick way for persons to get into the Bible text. Most of your class time should be spent on Dimensions 2 and 3.
- If participants do not work on Dimension 1 questions beforehand, you may want to allow them a brief amount of time to read the recommended Bible passage and to answer Dimension 1 questions, either individually or in teams.
- Discussions of Dimension 1 questions might lead you in these directions:
  1. Job 1:1-5 tells us that the man Job was blameless and upright, one who feared God, one who turned away from evil, a father (seven sons and three daughters), a person of wealth (thousands of cattle and many servants), and one who offered daily burnt offerings.
  2. Job's response when he lost everything was to tear his robe and shave his head. He fell on the ground and worshiped God, saying, "Naked I came from my mother's womb, and naked shall I return there; the LORD gave, and the LORD has taken away; blessed be the name of the LORD." Job asked, "Shall we receive the good at the hand of God, and not receive the bad?" He "did not sin with his lips."
  3. Job wished he had never been born.
  4. God responded to Job's friends: "My wrath is kindled against you . . . ; for you have not spoken of me what is right, as my servant Job has." God then tells them to take "seven bulls and seven rams" and offer a burnt offering.

(C) Compare Bible translations.

- Ahead of class time collect as many different versions of the Bible as you can. Try to have a King James Version, a New International Version, a *Good News Bible*, and a New Revised Standard Version.
- Distribute the different translations to class members. Look at Job 1 and 2 and discuss these questions:

—What words are used to describe Job in 1:1, 8?
—What words are used to describe those who came to present themselves to God in 1:6 and 2:1?
—Do any of the versions have footnotes that give possible alternative translations for any of the words in Job 1–2?
—Discuss the effect the different translations have on your perception of who these characters are.

(D) Dramatize the story.

- Begin with Job 1:6 and end with Job's words in 3:1-5 and 11-13.
- Ask for volunteers to read the following parts (listed in the order of their appearance): the Narrator, the Lord, Satan, the four messengers, and Job's wife. Give your readers a few minutes to read their parts.
- Ask everyone to read 1:1-5 silently. Then ask the narrator to start reading at verse 6.

(E) Conduct a mock interview with the principal characters.

- Ask for five volunteers: (1) a reporter (or a talk show host) who will interview (2) the Lord, (3) Satan, (4) Job, and (5) Job's wife.
- Allow a few minutes for the volunteers to review their characters and prepare for the interview.
- Make sure each character has an opportunity to remark on what has been happening in Uz. The interviewer should press each of them to reveal *why* they did or said what they did in the story.
- After the interview is over, ask class members to discuss how they might have answered differently, and why. Would they have thought the characters had different motives than the volunteers who played the parts?
- Were there any surprises during the interview? Share these insights.

Dimension 2: What Does the Bible Mean?

(F) Explore the image of Satan in the Old Testament.

- Read the article, "The Origin of Evil and the Figure of the Satan" (page 6 in this leader's guide). Present this information in a summary fashion to your class members.
- Divide class members into four groups. Each group will work with one of the Scripture passages listed below. Give each group the following information for its passage:
—**Group 1:** Look at the story of Balaam and his donkey in Numbers 22:21-33. Notice the word translated "as his adversary" or "as an adversary" (in the RSV and NRSV) in verses 22 and 32 (NIV says "to oppose him/you"). Lit-

erally, this phrase says "as a *satan* to him/to you." Reread both verses, substituting the phrase "as a *satan*" in the correct place in both verses.

—**Group 2:** Look at Psalm 109:6-7. Decide which English word translates the Hebrew word *satan* in these verses. (The word *accuser* in verse 6 represents the Hebrew word *satan*.) Reread the text, substituting the words "a satan" in the correct place.

—**Group 3:** Look at 1 Kings 11:14, 23, and 25 where RSV and NRSV use "adversary" to translate *satan*.

—**Group 4:** Look at Zechariah 3:1-2 and 1 Chronicles 21:1.

● Give the groups the following directions:

—Discuss what the role of the *satan* seems to be in each of these passages.

—What relationship does the *satan* have to God in each text?

—How does the function the *satan* plays in 1 Chronicles 21:1 differ from his function in the other passages?

(G) Take a closer look at Hebrew poetic structures.

● Review the information presented in the article "The Wisdom Literature and the Poetry of Israel" on pages 3–4 of the study book.

● A closer study of Hebrew literary style can help us better understand the richness of the Bible. We must always remember that the writers of the Bible used the writing styles of their day to convey these important stories, words, events of God.

● Hebrew poetry depends on the "rhyming" of ideas rather than sounds. Each verse of poetry consists of two or more parallel lines. The ideas in one line are echoed, modified, or amplified by the ideas in the following line or lines.

● To illustrate this concept, ask one person to read aloud Job 3:16-19.

● On the chalkboard or on a large piece of paper plot the parallel phrases in each verse.

Synonymous Parallelism

3:16 Why was I not buried like ⎡ a stillborn child
⎣ an infant that never sees the light

● Point out that 3:16 is an example of "synonymous parallelism" (see the definition in the article). The terms "stillborn child" and "infant that never sees the light" mean approximately the same thing.

● Draw a line from "child" to "infant" and from "stillborn" to "never sees the light."

● Discuss how the parallel phrases *differ* from each other. (If discussion lags, point out that the second line is less general or more specific than the first. The first phrase is an overall viewpoint: the child is born dead. The second narrows in on a specific aspect of this: the child born dead, never sees the light.)

Antithetical Parallelism

3:17 There ⎡ the wicked cease from troubling
⎣ the weary are at rest

● Point out that 3:17 is an example of contrasting or "antithetical" (an-tuh-THET-uh-cal) parallel lines. The wicked and the weary mean approximately opposite things. The wicked are the ones who do the troubling. The weary are the ones who have been troubled. Taken together, the two parts of the verse say that even the opposing sides of humanity (both the wicked and the weary) will have a reversal of their situations in death.

● If you have time, do the same type of analysis with verse 18 (in which the parallel terms are synonymous), before going on to explain the parallelism in verse 19.

3:18 There ⎡ the prisoners are at ease together
⎣ they do not hear the voice of the taskmaster

● Point out that "at ease" is a broad general statement. The second line is more specific. Prisoners can be at ease if "they do not hear the voice of the taskmaster."

Synthetic Parallelism

In this form of "thought rhyme" a new idea is added in the second line, over and beyond the ideas expressed in the first line.

● Look at Job 3:19. The ideas expressed in the two lines of 3:19 are not precisely parallel. However, "small" and "great" in the first line are more specifically said to be "slaves" and "masters" in the second line.

Here the idea of "being freed" in the second line does not echo anything in the first line but is introduced as a new thought.

● Discuss briefly: Does knowing something about the usual structure of Hebrew poetry affect your understanding of this material?

Dimension 3: What Does the Bible Mean to Us?

(H) Reflect on ways Christians react to suffering and loss.

● Divide class members into small groups with no more than three or four people in each group. These personal experiences will only be shared within each small group. Allow people time to gather in different corners of the room.

● Be aware that this type of personal sharing is very important and does take class time. Walk around to the groups, not to listen, but to check and see that everyone has "air" time to share their experiences. Know that all people do not feel comfortable with this type of personal sharing. Always allow people the option to "pass" in the sharing time.

- Ask the groups the following questions:
—Have you ever been called on to "comfort" or to respond to someone else when he or she had experienced a devastating loss? What did you say? Why?
—Have you had any times in your life when you felt like Job does in Chapter 3 (he wishes he had not been born)?
—How did other people respond to you at those times? What did friends, family, fellow church members, or people in helping professions say to you? How did their advice make you feel? Better? Worse? Did their words make you feel guilty (as though you were doing something wrong), or did they make you feel even more free to express your innermost thoughts?
- Call everyone back together. Job offers us several models of response when tragedy strikes. Ask the whole class these questions for general discussion:
—What are the benefits and what are the problems associated with Job's first type of response ("The LORD gave, the LORD has taken away") in 1:21?
—What are the benefits and the problems associated with Job's second type of response (his lament)?

(I) Look at contemporary funeral services.

- Before your class meets, see if you can find out what Scripture passages are often used for funerals in your church. Ask your pastor what passages he or she usually uses, obtain funeral service bulletins, or locate liturgies for funerals in *The United Methodist Book of Worship* (The United Methodist Publishing House, 1992; pages 139–171).

    This activity will help your class begin to look at Scripture passages as an important component of nurture and care during times of crisis and tragedy.
- List the Scripture passages used for funerals on the chalkboard or on a large piece of paper for class members to see. For each passage listed discuss:
—What is the purpose of including this text in a funeral?
—What does this text counsel or encourage mourners to think or to do?
—Does this text offer comfort?
- Now look at the models of response to tragedy that Job offers.
- Ask people to imagine this scenario: Your children are killed by a drunken driver. The funeral service (prepared by the pastor) uses Job 1:21 as one of its texts.
- Discuss: How would you feel when you heard this passage read? Would it make you feel better? Worse? Guilty? Resigned to your losses?
- Next, ask people to imagine that they have a painful, terminal illness. The chaplain who comes to visit them in the hospital reads Job 3:20-26 to them.
- Discuss: How would you feel when you heard this passage read in such a setting?

Another Scripture passage that is often used in times of tragedy is 1 Peter 4:12-19. This passage has sometimes been understood to say that complaining of the trials that come in one's life is a refusal to share in the sufferings of Christ. However, 1 Peter 4:19 implies that not all kinds of suffering are "in accordance with God's will."
- Discuss: Does Job suffer according to God's will? Could Job's complaint in Chapter 3 be seen as a form of "entrusting" himself to God?

(J) Find out what kind of a God this is.

- Read aloud Job 1:6-12. Pose this question to class members: Who was to blame for all Job's misfortunes?
- Did anyone say that God was the source of Job's misfortunes? If so, discuss reasons for saying this. If not, pose the question yourself: Might one say that God was ultimately to blame for all Job's misfortunes?
- Divide class members into small groups to discuss:
—Does the story in Job reflect the reality of God? (Is this really the way God behaves?) What makes you think so or not?
—If you do not think the story of Job reflects the reality of God, then what do you think does? How do you think God really does act, and why do you think so?
—How do you account for the misfortunes that have occurred in your own life? in the lives of others?

(K) Close the session with prayer.

- Ask everyone to join hands. Allow some time for silent prayer, but also invite those who wish to offer to God names of individuals, events, or world situations where suffering is present. Be sensitive to including global situations. So often we feel overwhelmed by the evil in our world. God is able to hear our concerns and our struggles with these overpowering situations.
- You may choose to close with this prayer by Dietrich Bonhoeffer:

    O merciful God,
    forgive me all the sins that I have committed
    against you and against my fellow men.
    I trust in your grace
    and commit my life wholly into your hands.
    Do with me according to your will
    and as is best for me.
    Whether I live or die, I am with you,
    and you, my God, are with me.
    Lord, I wait for your salvation
    and for your kingdom.

    Amen.[1]

[1] From *Prayers from Prison* by Dietrich Bonhoeffer, copyright © 1978 by Fortress Press. Used by permission of Augsburg Fortress.

Additional Bible Helps

The Origin of Evil and the Figure of the Satan
The Bible indicates that the religion of Israel changed over the course of Israel's long history as the people of God. One of the most obvious changes occurred with relationship to Israel's beliefs concerning the origins of evil.

Israelites apparently were familiar with the myths of the ancient Near Eastern cultures among whom they lived. Biblical poetic texts, in particular, make figurative references to the hostile powers of chaos who opposed the efforts of the Creator God before creation. These hostile powers are variously called Sea, River, the Deep/Deeps, Leviathan, Dragon, Rahab, and Serpent (said to have seven heads). The mythical monsters of chaos were thought to have been vanquished and restrained but not destroyed by the Creator God. Thus some texts speak as if evil in the world occurs when the forces of chaos escape the limits God has placed upon them. Echoes of these chaos-monster images can be found in Job 3:8; 7:12; 9:8, 13; 26:12; 38:8-11, as well as in Psalm 74:12-17; Psalm 89:9-14; Isaiah 27:1; 51:9-11; Daniel 7:11-14; Habakkuk 3:8-15.

Sometimes these mythological images are also made historical and applied to the earthly, political enemies of Israel, as in Isaiah 17:12-14; 30:7; or Jeremiah 51:34. The biblical authors need not have believed in the myths in order to make effective use of this imagery. Just as modern scientists need not believe in Greek myths in order to name a spaceship after Apollo, so ancient poets could borrow from the pool of imaginative language available in their culture in order to speak about such weighty issues as the relationship between God and evil.

By the time that the New Testament book known as The Revelation to John was written, these ancient chaos monsters had become associated with another figure known either as the Devil or the Satan (Revelation 12:9).

In Hebrew, the term *satan* comes from a root meaning "that which opposes, accuses, or creates a barrier." In Greek, the word *diabolos* (devil) has the similar meaning of "accuser" or "slanderer." New Testament writers use either "Satan" or "the Devil" to refer to the cosmic source of evil, the archenemy of God. However, the Satan is usually understood in quite a different way in Old Testament texts.

In most Old Testament texts "the Satan" is pictured as an administrative agent, working under God's supervision. "The Satan" is humankind's opponent, not God's opponent. It is the Satan's duty to test the loyalty of those who claim to love the Lord (Job 1–2 and Zechariah 3:1-9).

In many Old Testament texts it is the Lord (rather than the Satan) who is the source of both human joys and human sorrows (for example, Isaiah 45:7). In 1 Samuel 16:14-23 it is said to be the Lord who sends an evil spirit to torment Saul and in 1 Kings 22:18-28 the Lord is said to send "a lying spirit" to deceive Ahab.

But a comparison of 2 Samuel 24:1-25 and 1 Chronicles 21:1-30 indicates that over time, the people of Israel began to associate the deceptive aspects of God's actions with "the Satan." Both passages recount the same historical incident (David's census-taking). However, the history that was written before the Exile says it was the Lord who prompted David to take the census (2 Samuel 24:1), while the postexilic historian known as the Chronicler says it was "the Satan" who "incited David to count the people of Israel" (1 Chronicles 21:1).

When we compare Old Testament and New Testament ideas about the spread of evil in the world, we can see that some further changes in people's thinking occurred in the intertestamental period (in between the writing of the last of the Old Testament books, around 200 B.C., and the writing of the first of the New Testament books, around A.D. 100). In this period (about which we know very little), "the Satan" became an increasingly powerful and sinister character in the eyes of the people descended from Abraham. During the so-called Intertestamental Period, the Satan who was once thought of as the Lord's servant developed into an independent power in competition with the Lord.

No biblical texts explain exactly how this distinct change in the Satan's image came about. But the reference in The Revelation to John to a "war" in heaven that led to the defeat of "the dragon and his angels" (12:7-9) seems to have led to the development of a popular Christian legend. The legend says the Devil (or Satan) was a "fallen angel," who was cast out of heaven after his excessive pride led him to rebel against God.

In order to read the story of Job in an appropriate manner, we must constantly remind ourselves that the Satan pictured by the narrator in Job 1–2 is not guilty of infidelity to the Lord. The Satan does not tempt Job to sin. He merely sets up a test by which Job's loyalty to God may be proved (or disproved). We must not paint him with a brush that only fits his later image. As you read Job, remember that the Satan in this story is a member of the heavenly court, *not* an independent cosmic force in opposition to the power of the Lord.

Planning ahead . . .
The Book of Job opens up important subjects for discussion. During the weeks your class is studying Job you might want to plan a class social or a dinner/study event. You could use this additional time together to delve more deeply into the materials offered in the leader's guide and study book. Or you might want to have dinner together and view the movie *Shadowlands* (1993, Savoy Pictures, Inc.).

Shadowlands is the autobiographical telling of C. S. Lewis and his wife Joy's life together. Be especially tuned in for the movement of Lewis's theology regarding suffering and pain.

2 "With Friends Like These..."

Job 4:7-19;
5:17-27; 8:1-7;
18:1-21; 11:13-20;
20:1-19; 13:1-12;
21:7-34

LEARNING MENU

As you plan this session, remember that the Book of Job, and especially this section of the book, will remind people of their own times of crisis, of what people said to them during those times (or what they wish people had said), and how they came to understand their relationship with God through that crisis. These are difficult and sensitive subjects and need to be handled with care, especially if your group is newly formed or has someone in it who is newly bereaved. Do not push people to share more than they are readily willing to do.

Remember that Job's friends are *not* good models of how we ought to respond to friends or loved ones in times of loss and grief. But we can learn a great deal from this book about what is *not* helpful to say to people who are experiencing pain.

Keeping in mind the ways your class members learn best, as well as their needs and interests, choose at least one learning segment from each of the three Dimensions.

Dimension 1: What Does the Bible Say?

(A) Share in an opening worship time.

- Begin your class time together with a few moments of silence. You may want to ask people to remember or to name events of suffering they have become aware of during the week. Close your time with this Psalm reading:

> "Hear my prayer, O LORD,
>   and give ear to my cry;
>   do not hold your peace at my tears.
> For I am your passing guest,
>   an alien, like all my forebears.
> Turn your gaze away from me,
>   that I may smile again,
>   before I depart and am no more."
> —Psalm 39:12-13

(B) Answer Dimension 1 questions in the study book.

- Discussion of the questions may lead you in these directions:
  1. Eliphaz says those who cultivate evil will reap the

same and that by the "breath of God they perish." By a blast of God's anger "they are consumed."

2. Bildad counsels Job to make supplications to the Almighty. "If you are pure and upright," he says, God will restore you to your rightful place. And "your latter days will be very great." Zophar counsels Job to direct his heart rightly and stretch out his hands to God, to rid himself of wickedness, to forget his misery, and to have hope and courage.

3. In Job's experience the wicked often go unpunished. These verses give many examples of how the wicked live long, full lives and how "no rod of God is upon them."

> **Advance preparation**
> Many readers will find the poetic speeches in Job difficult to understand. It will help if the leader or a volunteer from the class can prepare or look at a paraphrase, a summary, or a simplified version of the assigned texts ahead of time. One very good simplified text is *The Book of Job* translated and with an introduction by Stephen Mitchell (North Point Press, San Francisco, 1987). This version appeared in an earlier edition called *Into the Whirlwind* (Doubleday, 1979), which may still be available in some libraries.

(C) Take a closer look at Job's friends.

- Split class members into three groups. Assign Bildad to one group, Eliphaz to another, and Zophar to the third group.
- Ask each group to characterize the kind of responses that its character gave to Job in its assigned Scripture passages.
— Focus on these Scripture passages for your work: Eliphaz (4:7-19 and 5:17-27), Bildad (8:1-7 and 18:1-21), Zophar (11:13-20 and 20:1-19).
- Choose one of the following ways to characterize the friends' responses:
— Ask the groups to compile a list of scriptural quotations from their character, quotations that represent accurately his responses to Job.
— Ask the groups to give a "verbal mugshot" of their character by simply describing his point of view in responding to Job.
— Instead of using quotations directly from the text, ask the groups to paraphrase their character's responses by making up their own quotations for him. These made-up responses might include some of the "easy answers" we tend to hear when we are being "consoled" by our friends. For example, the group describing Eliphaz might have him saying to Job, "just go to God in prayer."
— Groups might also be given the option to choose one of the above methods, or to make up their own way to describe their character.

(D) Hold a trial: "Job vs. God."

Option One: Divide class members into pairs, and ask them to work as Job's defense lawyers. The pairs should be given only five to ten minutes in which to prepare Job's defense before his accusing friends.

- Ask each pair to compile a summary of Job's reasons for thinking he is innocent, in light of his friends' accusations. Tell the groups to remember that neither Job nor his friends know the first part of the story (the prose narrative found in Chapters 1–2). As far as Job and his friends are concerned, God's "deal" with the adversary is nothing but conjecture and so is not an admissible piece of evidence.
- After the pairs have prepared their brief defense statements, list on a chalkboard or large piece of paper the various defenses the different groups prepared for Job.

Option Two: Divide class members into different pairs, and ask them to prepare Job's "indictment" of God. They can begin by reading Job 23:4 in which Job states his wish to lay his case before God.

- Ask the groups to prepare summary indictments stating what exactly is Job's case against God. The groups might want to make these serious or funny, strictly out of Scripture or filled with legal jargon.
- After five to ten minutes, let pairs share their statements with the rest of the class.

Dimension 2: What Does the Bible Mean?

(E) Make your own "Glossary" for the Book of Job.

- You will need at least two Bible concordances for this option.
- Two terms that are important for better understanding the Book of Job are *retribution theology* and *Sheol*. (Feel free to add other terms that may concern your class.)
- Divide class members into three small groups to study *retribution theology* and *Sheol*.
— Group 1 can use the definitions in the study book (pages 14, 16).
— Group 2 can look up the biblical texts mentioned in the study book to find where retribution theology is described elsewhere in the Old Testament (Deuteronomy 7:12-15; Joshua 23:16; Psalm 1:6; Proverbs 3:9-10; 13:9; Jeremiah 31:29-30; Ezekiel 18:1-20). For *Sheol*, tell the group to use a concordance to look up some of the references to Sheol found elsewhere in the Old Testament. (This group cannot be expected to do an exhaustive search, but it can at least gain a sampling of the word's use, which will prove helpful.)

—Group 3 can look for statements indicating retribution theology in the Book of Job, which are mostly contained *not* in the words of Job but in the words of his friends. Also ask this group to look in a Bible concordance for references to Sheol found in the Book of Job.
- After the groups have finished their work, let them share their information in a group discussion aimed at refining their understanding of retribution theology and Sheol.
- To conclude the discussion, summarize and present the information about Sheol found in the article on "Popular Theology in Wisdom Literature and Psalms," page 70. Be sure to emphasize that Sheol does not conform to modern ideas about "Hell." No Old Testament references ever associate Sheol with fire, heat, or pain. Sheol was considered the state of being dead, the place where everyone went after death. It was never understood to be a place where any kind of punishment took place after death.

(F) Search Job's "comforters' " words.

One thing we can learn from the Book of Job is what *not* to say to someone else when we are trying to give comfort in times of crisis and pain. We find out by the end of Job that not even God approves of the opinions of Job's friends. The answers that the friends see as right—the answers that are right from the point of view of their culture—are not right in God's eyes. If you choose this option you will want to follow it up with the discussion suggested in option "H," because people will probably notice that many of the comments made by Job's friends are things that we are told by individuals or by religion in our own times of crisis and pain.
- Ask the whole class to search the Eliphaz, Bildad, and Zophar sections to find verses that remind them of "consoling remarks" they themselves have heard or used. Write the results on the board or flipchart. If you also choose to do option "H," this listing will come in handy for comparison.
- End this section by asking class members if anyone remembers what Job's advice to his friends was. What was it that Job would have found helpful from them in the situation? (In 13:1-12, Job criticizes the words of his friends, telling them that the wisest response they could have offered in this situation would have been silence, 13:5.)

(G) Describe some understandings of God.

- Divide class members into pairs to discuss the understandings of God presented in this section of Job. They should compile scripturally based characterizations of God from both Job's point of view and from the friends' points of view. After the pairs have worked for a while,

ask them to contribute to a class characterization of God from these differing points of view. Once your list has been made and posted in a place where the whole class can look at it, compare and discuss these understandings of God. Your discussion may include these questions:
—Do Job's friends have different assumptions about God than Job does? If so, what are those assumptions?
—What kind of a title might Job give God, and what kind of a title might Job's friends give God?
—How do Job and his friends differ in their understandings of God's power, love, mercy, and forgiveness?

Dimension 3:
What Does the Bible Mean to Us?

(H) Examine what we say to friends in times of pain.

- If you chose to do option "F," this option will make a nice follow-up. Acknowledge from the beginning that Job's friends were not very helpful to him in the midst of his crisis and pain. Suggest that some of us may also have received well-meant but essentially uncomforting counsel from our friends or from religious doctrines in times of crisis. Ask class members to make another list, this time not out of the Scripture, but out of their own lives. Ask people to discuss:
—What are the comments you have heard (either from individuals or from religious organizations) that were less than helpful in times of crisis? (It will be important here to respect individual opinions, since one person may find the comment "it's all for the best" helpful while another may find it aggravating. This may depend on the situation in which the comment was made or it may depend on what the individual caught up in that situation believes about God.) Expect for people to disagree, and encourage an attitude of openness to different opinions.
- Be sure to allow time for people to explain their additions to the list so others can understand their point of view.
- Taking a cue from what Job says in Chapter 13, ask class members to discuss whether being quietly present is a helpful or comforting thing to do. Is this how we would prefer our friends to respond to us in times of crisis and pain? What in fact would we prefer people say to us in their attempts at consolation? Let this discussion develop into the making of one more list, one of *good* or comforting things people have said to you or that you have heard said to others that you think would be comforting to you. Again, remember that opinions about this will vary from person to person and from situation to situation. Give people a chance to explain their contributions to the list and, if they so choose, to share the situations that taught them to feel that way.

- Close with a prayer asking for guidance when we are called upon to comfort a friend and for patience when we are counseled by well-intentioned but not very helpful friends.

(I) Look closer at anti-retribution theology.

Job had the courage (or perhaps the foolhardiness) to risk speaking out against the commonly believed retributive theology of his time. Job will later be supported by the writer of Ecclesiastes. Both Job and Ecclesiates observe (and state out loud) that sometimes the wicked do prosper and sometimes the righteous do suffer.

- Ask class members to pair off and look first at Ecclesiastes 7:15 and then at Job's retributive theology-blasting remarks in Chapter 21.
- Ask the pairs to discuss their own personal observations. Do they think that bad things sometimes happen to good people (as Rabbi Harold S. Kushner assumes in the title of his book, *When Bad Things Happen to Good People*; Schocken Books, 1981), or do they tend to believe in retributive theology?
- Ask the pairs to use personal experiences in their discussions to whatever degree they feel comfortable.
—If Job and Ecclesiastes are right and Job's friends are wrong, then what does this say about the nature of God?
—If the wicked are not punished and the just are not rewarded, how then do we understand God to be just? (You may want to summarize and share the article in the "Additional Bible Helps," page 12, on the many ways people have tried to answer this question of God's justice.)
- If your class is comfortable enough with one another, get back in the larger group and ask if anyone would like to share some of the issues they discussed within their pairs. Make sure this is a time of safe discussion for anyone who wishes to share and a time in which anyone who prefers not to share can feel comfortable being silent. Following this discussion, ask one of the class members to give a closing prayer.

(J) Discuss some understandings of God.

(If you chose to use option "G," this option will be a nice follow-up.)
- Split the class in half. Assign one half the theology, or understanding of God, represented by Job and the other half the theology of Job's friends.
- Then present them with a problem of evil. This problem could be one everybody is likely to be familiar with, like the Holocaust or the April 19, 1995, bombing of the Alfred P. Murrah Federal Building in Oklahoma City, Oklahoma. Other options for the discussion of evil might be of natural evil like a nearby tornado or a local child with a terminal illness. Be careful to not pick a topic that will put one or two people in particular on the spot.
- Having presented the problem, each group should answer the following questions from the point of view of the character or characters (Job/his friends) it has been assigned:
—How is God related to this problem? Why has this evil occurred?
—How do you view God in light of this situation?
—How do you view yourself in light of this situation?
- Ask the groups to argue their positions back and forth for a while, airing as much of their character's opinion as possible.
- Close by asking class members which of these theologies they identify with more closely. Further, ask if the discussion about Job and his friends' understandings of God has changed, impacted, or reinforced their views of God, and how.

(K) Find out if you have the patience of Job.

Occasionally someone will use the phrase "the patience of Job" referring to someone who is very patient. Having become fairly familiar with the Book of Job, class members will probably acknowledge that Job is not particularly patient. He may be unwilling to reject God, but he certainly is not patient in his quest to understand his situation!

- Most of us have felt like Job at one time or another. Ask class members (together or in groups of five to eight, if the class is too large) to discuss aspects of Job's experience and specific comments he makes that remind them of their own lives.
—What about Job really strikes a familiar chord, and why?
—What are some of Job's comments that could have come from their own mouths?
—Does Job say anything you have sometimes wished you could say (things you have thought but did not dare to say out loud)?
- Try to give everyone an opportunity to share.
- Close the class by giving everyone paper and pen. Choose one of the two following activities:
—Ask persons to write a short letter to Job, expressing their feelings about his experience. These feelings might be of empathy, or they might be of exasperation. The point is to have class members tell Job whatever is on their minds at the moment.
—Ask persons to write a letter to God in which they can ask their own Job-like (impatient) questions, state their complaints, sing God's praises, or whatever they feel compelled to write.

(L) Hold a closing worship.

Hopefully this session will have raised some difficult questions and led to some heart-searching discussions. The closing moments of worship will be an important time to pull together the threads of the day's discussion. Try to recapture these ideas and questions.
- If you have a copy of Harold Kushner's book *When Bad Things Happen to Good People* (Schocken Books, 1981) you might want to include the prayer on page 118 in this closing worship time.

Additional Bible Helps

Theodicy: The Question of God's Justice

Many biblical passages claim (or assume) that God rewards the righteous and punishes those who do evil. This belief is expressed in a particularly forceful way in the Deuteronomic tradition (Deuteronomy, Joshua, Judges, Kings) and in the Book of Proverbs. It is also this belief that acts as a foundation for many of the Psalms. But human experience suggests otherwise; in real life it often seems to the careful observer that the innocent do suffer, while the evil prosper.

The problem we encounter when we believe in a God of justice and yet see that injustices continue to happen on earth is sometimes called "theodicy." This term comes from the Greek words for God (*theos*) and justice (*dika*). The horrible suffering of an innocent man in the Book of Job raises a question in our minds about the justice of God. Job poses an interesting problem, for he is a man that even God acknowledges as innocent: "There is no one like him on earth, a blameless and upright man who fears God and turns away from evil" (Job 1:8); yet God allows Job to suffer.

Theodicy asks the question: If God is all-powerful and all-good, why does God allow innocent people to suffer? By definition, an all-powerful God could control or even prevent suffering. But if the innocent still suffer in our world then God either cannot be all-powerful, or God cannot be good and just. If God is good and just and yet people still suffer, then it seems that God must not be all-powerful.

We can understand the problem of theodicy through a simple equation of three statements, all of which cannot be logically true at the same time: God is good, God is omnipotent, and innocent people suffer. Logically, it seems that in order to affirm that God is a just God, one must deny or qualify the truth of one of these three statements. People have tried to resolve this theological and logical dilemma in a variety of ways. Naturally, evil does not fit nicely into one theological category. But hopefully the following views will be helpful in continuing to address theodicy in our modern world.

A *theodicy of protest* questions God's goodness, asking why an all-powerful God would allow the slaughter of children, the Holocaust, and other atrocities. If God were good, God would answer prayers of help, which seem to be ignored. A protest theodicy can be found in Psalms of lament, such as Psalms 13, 35, 74, 82, 89, 90, and 94, when the psalmist asks, "How long, O LORD? Will you forget me forever? / How long must I bear pain in my soul?"

Process theodicy maintains that God is good but questions the nature of God's power, claiming that God's power is persuasive rather than absolute and that there is evil that is outside of God's control. God simply does not have the power to prevent all tragedies and suffering. Nevertheless, God is a constant influence for ultimate good. Process theodicy is popular among those who hold fast to the goodness of God, but it has relatively little scriptural basis.

Free-will theodicy claims that because God gave humans the freedom to choose between right and wrong, our suffering is a result of our own choices for evil. This theodicy fails to account for the suffering caused by events outside of human control, such as floods, earthquakes, famine, and disease. (Some refer to this type of evil as "natural" evil.)

An *educative theodicy* claims that suffering is ultimately good because it provides an opportunity for growth. Suffering deepens character, strengthens compassion, and nurtures creativity, as well as increases our appreciation for good. However, people do not necessarily have to suffer in order to achieve these characteristics, and this theodicy ignores the fact that many people are completely destroyed by their suffering. Ultimate human growth cannot be justified easily by the waste of life.

An *eschatological theodicy* claims that if people experience compensation after death for evil suffered in life, then their suffering is not in vain. The promise of a just reward received in an after-life (end-time, or eschaton [ES-kuh-tahn]) is a comfort to many who suffer, but it is often used as an excuse for failure to remedy unjust situations in this life and subjugates people to lifetimes of oppression. Placing all hope in a future of bliss negates the possibility of living life to the fullest in the present.

A *theodicy of mystery* emphasizes the inability of human beings to understand God's purposes. Many times Christians are taught to trust in a theodicy of the mystery of God's goodness and mercy, having blind faith that God's purpose will triumph over evil. While this is a popular theodicy, it diminishes the capacity for human relationship with God. People are seen to be more like pawns in a cosmic chess game than creatures called to responsibility and relationship with God.

In a *theodicy of communion*, Christians have identified the suffering of Jesus as God's own suffering with humanity. Through willing suffering for others, humans have the opportunity for a deeper intimacy with God. However, even the redemptive quality of suffering for others (based on the suffering servant of Isaiah 53 and Jesus as Messiah) can be misused if it glorifies suffering and invites victims to remain passive in the face of evil.

3 "Where Were You When I Laid the Foundation of the Earth?"

Job 38–42

LEARNING MENU

Keeping in mind the ways your class members learn best, as well as their needs and interests, choose at least one learning segment from each of the three Dimensions.

Dimension 1: What Does the Bible Say?

(A) Hold an opening worship.

- Ask class members to stand in a circle and to take turns mentioning the names of people or situations that are of concern to them.
- An appropriate hymn to end this time would be stanza 1 of "Amazing Grace" (*The United Methodist Hymnal*, 378).

(B) Answer the questions in the study book.

- Ask class members to discuss their answers to all four questions as a group. Use a chalkboard and chalk or a large piece of paper and a marker to jot down the variety of answers.

1. Be sure people note the verbatim similarity of 38:3a to 40:7a. Then help them to list other similarities and differences of the verses, drawing on the answers they gave in the study book. Once everyone in the class has had a chance to give input, ask them to note similarities and differences brought up by others that they had not noticed before.
2. Point out that the second question requires a comparison of concepts and ideas rather than words.
3. Let answers given to the third question become a springboard for some larger exploration of ancient Near Eastern views of creation. Far from being just poetic descriptions of the world, these verses in Job portray an understanding of the universe that was common to most people of the ancient Near East. Genesis 1, a number of the Psalms, and the Book of Job all have slightly different pictures of how the universe is constructed and how it operates. Note that Job 38 talks about the "foundation of the earth" (38:4-6), conjuring up pictures of an earth-structure balanced on supports of some sort. Light is pictured as if it acts like an animated being (38:12-15); the "gates of death" are thought to lie beneath the "deeps" (38:16-17). Job 38:22-27 pictures the way different kinds of precipitation might be stored and properly distributed. Finally, 38:31-33 explains the movement of the planets and the stars in their constellations.

13

Jews as well as Babylonians and Assyrians shared some of the same understandings of how the universe was constructed. If your class has studied Genesis together in this series, you might find some of these descriptions familiar.

4. As you go over this question, help class members stick with a short answer to the question, stating that Job made his daughters inheritors, "along with" his sons. Briefly discuss the implications of finding this statement at the end of Job. Usually, sons were the only heirs, and thus Job's treatment of his daughters was strange (to say the least). Try to save further discussion of this topic for later (option "J").

(C) Outline the structure of Job.

- Use the information in the "Additional Bible Helps," page 16, to help class members get an overview of what they have and have not studied in the Book of Job.
- Draw a sort of "timeline" and have the class break the Book of Job into logical sections, noting the chapters involved in each. It would be good to note the introduction, the debate (which could be broken down into speakers), the speeches of Elihu, God's answer from the whirlwind, Job's answer, and the conclusion.
- This might be something the class members would want to copy onto a small sheet of paper or directly into their Bibles at the beginning of Job for future reference.

(D) Find the missing links/pieces in Job.

- Also related to the structure of Job is the issue of how the book was put together, or edited.
- Ask the class to imagine that they will be involved in making a movie version of the Book of Job. Their particular task is to act as "continuity editors," people who look for missing pieces, inconsistencies, and other problems in continuity in the "screenplay" (which for our purposes is the present biblical form of the book).
- Ask class members to get into "editing teams" and to make a list of whatever continuity problems they can see. (For instance, Satan disappears without explanation, or God in the whirlwind speech at the end does not acknowledge the pact with Satan made in the beginning of the story, and so on).
- Call class members back together as an "editorial board" to report the problems they have found. (Assure the class members they are not going to be given the task of fixing these editorial problems. At this stage, it is simply important to note them).

Dimension 2: What Does the Bible Mean?

(E) Debate this question: Does God's response provide a satisfactory answer to Job's questions?

- God's speech from the whirlwind is a response to Job, but is it an answer? Does it provide Job with a way to understand what has been happening to him? Opinions vary on this.
- First clarify what you think Job's question was. Ask the class to state the main question Job hoped God would answer (something to the effect of, "why have these bad things happened to me, a righteous person?").
- Then divide class members into two groups, place them on opposite sides of the room or table, and ask them to debate the issue.
—Tell one group their job is to argue that God *did* in fact answer Job's question. They will have to make up their own arguments, but the goal is to argue effectively that God did give an adequate answer to Job.
—Tell the other group to prepare to argue, in their own words, that God did *not* answer Job, in terms of actually responding to his question about the way God works.
- Depending on the size of the groups, you might give them some preliminary time to develop their "cases" and encourage them to appoint a main spokesperson. Then, let the debate begin.
- When the sides have presented their main arguments and have had the chance to respond to one another's accusations and questions, allow time for closing statements and end the debate.
- Then, ask the class members to choose the side that is most convincing to them personally and to move to that side of the room or that side of the table that presented their personal point of view in the debate.
- Ask people to share why they do or do not think God answered Job's question, and whether their original points of view were at all affected by the arguments given in this debate.

(F) Use a process of elimination to clarify God's answers.

Whether or not God answered Job's question, God does make some specific statements about what is NOT the answer to Job's question. By examining what God rejects, we can find out a great deal.

- Present this concept to the class and ask them to look for the things God rejects as being true.
- Write these things on the chalkboard or a large piece of

paper, along with citations of each chapter and verse.
- If answers are slow in coming, remind people (for example) that in 42:7-9 the Lord condemns Eliphaz and his friends for not saying what was right about God to Job. Then ask:
—What answer does God reject when God says Eliphaz and his friends have not said what is right about God?
—Or remind people that in Chapters 38–41 the Lord makes it clear that Job's responses have not been so right, either.
—What was it that Job was wrong about?
- In Chapters 38–41, the Lord is explicit in mentioning many other aspects of creation aside from humans. What does this indicate that Job and his friends were wrong about? (They assume that they, as humans, were so all-important that God would be mostly occupied with watching, judging, punishing, and rewarding them.)

(G) Undertake an editorial investigation of Job 42:2-6.

Class members may have determined (possibly just by reading the study book) that 42:2-6 has some difficulties.
- Split class members into four groups and ask them to explore these difficulties and the answers.
—Ask Group 1 to read the explanation in the study book about this section ("Job Comes to a Decision," page 26).
—Ask Group 2 to look at the annotations in a few different study Bibles to see what answers they might offer.
—Ask Group 3 to explore one or two biblical commentaries on these verses (many church libraries have either a one-volume biblical commentary, or a set of commentaries covering the whole Bible).
—Ask Group 4 to use their own creative and intuitive wiles to gain understanding of this passage.
- When the groups are finished, let them report their findings to each other and discuss what (in light of all this information) they think the present (final) version of this passage means.

Dimension 3: What Does the Bible Mean to Us?

(H) Discuss the effect the Book of Job has had on you and your beliefs.

- At the very least, the study of the Book of Job should prompt personal reflection about God and what we believe about God. If your class is too large to have a whole group discussion (or if people do not feel completely comfortable with one another), divide up into groups of two or three for discussion purposes.
- Ask them to discuss some of the following questions:
—Does the Book of Job prompt you to question or to have second thoughts about anything you have previously been taught to believe about God? If so, what?
—Has the Book of Job made you think differently about the concepts of reward and punishment by God?
—Do you feel satisfied by God's answer to Job? Why, or why not?
—What questions would you like to have answered in a speech from the whirlwind?
—What do you think about the prospect of complaining to and/or about God now that you have read Job?
- Close with a group prayer in which class members are each asked to present either a question they have for God or to give thanks for an answer they feel they have received. As always, give people the freedom to pass (skip their turn) if they are not comfortable sharing their prayer with the rest of the group.

(I) Evaluate your pastoral counseling techniques in light of what you have learned from Job.

In the last session you may not have chosen the option that allowed people to discuss what comments they had found helpful or not helpful when they were experiencing times of pain and crisis in their own lives (options "F" and "H"). If you did not do this last week, this session would be a good time to investigate what you have learned from Job about crisis counseling.
- Ask your class for six volunteers to do three different roleplays.
- Ask one set of three volunteers to roleplay sufferers, people who are caught up in situations of tragedy and grief. These people are looking for answers to questions such as "Why is this happening to me?" or "Why did God let this happen?"
- Ask another set of three volunteers to roleplay "pastoral counselors" or "chaplains" who will suggest answers to the sufferers' questions, based on what they have learned from their study of the Book of Job.
- Have the first sufferer describe what has happened to him or her and ask his or her question. Have the first counselor give an answer to that question. Do the same with the second and third set of volunteers. Then open the discussion to include the whole class, and ask:
—Did any of the answers given resemble the answer the friends gave to Job? Why, or why not?
—Did any of the answers given resemble the answer God gave to Job from the whirlwind? Why, or why not?
—Which of the answers given by the volunteers seemed to be the most or the least comforting or helpful?
- To close, offer a prayer asking God to bless the words we offer to others the next time we are called upon to give counseling or comfort to a suffering person.

(J) Discuss Job's treatment of his daughters.

The study book mentions how unusual Job's decision to make his daughters co-inheritors of his property, along with their brothers, must have seemed in a society that often assumed that women could neither inherit nor own property.

Is it possible that Job's experience as one who was oppressed caused him to liberate his daughters from the oppression of the social customs of his time?

- Ask class members to discuss this issue in regard to the actual text, the feasibility of it, and so forth. But then move the question into their own lives.
- Make two lists on the board or a large piece of paper. One should be titled "oppressed who become liberators" and the other "oppressed who become oppressors."
- Ask class members to fill in these lists with examples of people they know and with people they might have to introduce and describe to the rest of the class.
- Then ask them to discuss what they think might be the difference between the people on the two lists.

—What causes some oppressed people to liberate others while some oppressed people oppress others?

- Up to this point, the conversation may well have been mostly about people not in the room. Now encourage the class members to include themselves in the conversation, or at least to consider their own placement on the lists.

—When have they been oppressed and become liberators, and when have they been oppressed and remained oppressors?

—What was the difference in the situations for them?

- Close by praying together for all who are oppressors, including ourselves. At this point offer a time of silence telling people to picture in their mind, during the silence, specific people they think of as oppressors and specific ways in which we ourselves are oppressors. Then, pray for all who are oppressed, including ourselves. Ask for the group to then pray silently for those they see as oppressed and to think of the ways in which we ourselves are oppressed.

(K) Illustrate what the author of Job sees to be God's priorities.

Part of what the Lord seems to be telling Job in the answer from the whirlwind is that neither he, nor the rest of humanity, occupies THE central place in the universe. God forcefully reminds Job that many other parts of creation have a claim on God's time and attention. God says to Job, "You are NOT the center of the universe."

- Present this idea to class members by making two charts. For this activity you will need two large pieces of paper and some markers.
- At the top of one chart draw a stick figure of one or more human beings.
- At the top of the other chart, put a variety of animals, trees, flowers, and so on, with a human being or two scattered among them at random.
- Ask class members to list ways in which we humans think and act as if we are the center of the universe. Write these ways at the top of the chart that has only human figures.
- Then list things that should help us remember that humans are not at the center of the universe. Write these at the top of the other chart.
- Then ask these questions:

—What might we do differently in our lives if we were really convinced that human beings are not the sole focus of God's love and creation?

—What might the God-speeches in Job have to say with regard to species that are endangered by human needs and developments?

- To close, ask class members to do an impromptu prayer litany, lifting up the other parts of the universe in which we live. Start by praying, "God, we give you praise for all you have created." Then go around the prayer circle, letting each class member add something: "God, we give you praise for . . ."
- Another good way to close would be by reading the children's book, *Brother Eagle, Sister Sky* (Susan Jeffers, Dial Books, 1991). It is told from a Native American point of view. This book lifts up all of creation as being connected and very important. If your group is small enough to see the illustrations while you read, have this be an eyes-open prayer, reminding people of our own need to keep our eyes open to all that is around us.

Additional Bible Helps

Reading Between the Prose in Job
In between the prose introduction and the prose conclusion to Job, we find two complete cycles and a third incomplete (or mangled) cycle of speeches between Job and his three friends, a set of four monologues by a character named Elihu, and the Lord's speeches, all written in poetic form.

A. The prose narrative beginning: Chapters 1–2
B. The First Cycle of Speeches:
 1. Job's first speech: Chapter 3
 2. Eliphaz's first speech: Chapters 4–5
 3. Job's reply: Chapters 6–7
 4. Bildad's first speech: Chapter 8
 5. Job's reply: Chapters 9–10
 6. Zophar's first speech: Chapter 11
 7. Job's reply: Chapters 12–14
C. The Second Cycle of Speeches:
 1. Eliphaz's second speech: Chapter 15
 2. Job's reply: Chapters 16–17
 3. Bildad's second speech: Chapter 18
 4. Job's reply: Chapter 19

5. Zophar's second speech: Chapter 20
   6. Job's reply: Chapter 21
D. The Third Cycle of Speeches:
   1. Eliphaz's third speech: Chapter 22
   2. Job's reply: Chapters 23–24
   3. Bildad's third speech: Chapter 25
   4. Job's reply: Chapter 26

There is nothing in the text as it comes down to us today to indicate that Zophar made a third speech or that Job replied a third time. However, some readers think that parts of Chapter 27 (such as 27:8-23) sound more like they should belong to Zophar than to Job. Zophar's name may have been dropped out of the text accidentally. But as the text has been handed down to us it seems that Chapters 27–31 contain two lengthy speeches by Job, both of which begin anew with the statement, "Job again took up his discourse and said" (27:1; 29:1).

If Chapter 27 is spoken by Job, then it seems to be directed toward all three of his friends, collectively. Chapter 28 contains a poem or hymn in praise of Wisdom. In Chapters 29–30, Job compares his present suffering with his previous prosperity and happiness.

Finally, in Chapter 31 Job swears an oath of innocence, using an oath formula that follows a pattern known to us from other Old Testament usages. The full pattern of such oaths includes both an "if" and a "then" statement: "If I have done such and such, then let thus and so happen to me in return" (see 31:7-8, 9-10, 16-22). It seems that Job is responding to the accusations his friends have made against him in their speeches. Chapter 31 concludes with an editorial statement: "the words of Job are ended." It is at this point that one would expect to find the Lord's response to Job.

Instead, 32:1-5 introduces the reader to a new character who has never before been mentioned in either the prose or the poetic materials. This new speaker, named Elihu, is said to be "angry at Job because he justified himself rather than God" (32:2) and angry "at Job's three friends because they had found no answer" to Job's arguments (32:3).

Elihu thinks he has come up with a better argument than Job's friends have been able to muster. He addresses four speeches in a row to Job. Each speech has an opening phrase that identifies Elihu as the speaker (32:6, 34:1, 35:1, 36:1). Elihu acknowledges the presence of the three friends, but he addresses most of his words to Job. However, Job does not respond to Elihu; and neither does the Lord, whose speeches begin immediately after Elihu's speeches end. The fact that both Job and the Lord seem to ignore the very existence of Elihu leads some readers to conclude that the Elihu speeches are a later intrusive addition to an earlier form of the book. An earlier form of the book probably moved directly from the end of Job's last speech to the Lord's response to Job (from the end of Chapter 31 to what is now the beginning of Chapter 38).

Finally, the voice from the whirlwind addresses Job directly. The Lord's first speech (in 38:1–40:2) ends with a demand that Job respond, but Job's response in 40:3-5 sounds more like a refusal to answer than an answer. The Lord's second speech (in 40:6–41:34) calls forth a more substantial answer from Job (42:1-6).

The following chart should help you visualize the summary given above:

E. The Job Monologues:
   1. Job speaks to his three friends: Chapter 27
   2. Job Praises Wisdom: Chapter 28
   3. Job reflects on his changed situation: Chapters 29–30
   4. Job swears to his innocence: Chapter 31
F. The Elihu Speeches
   1. Elihu's first speech: Chapters 32–33
   2. Elihu's second speech: Chapter 34
   3. Elihu's third speech: Chapter 35
   4. Elihu's fourth speech: Chapters 36–37
G. The Lord's Speeches and Job's Replies
   1. The Lord's first speech: Job 38:1–40:1
   2. Job's refusal to answer: Job 40:3-5
   3. The Lord's second speech: Job 40:6–41:34
   4. Job's final answer: Job 42:1-6
H. The Prose Narrative Ending: Job 42:7-17

4
Psalms 6; 30; 47; 150

Seasons of the Heart and Spirit

LEARNING MENU

We begin our study of Psalms by sampling a few of the many types of prayers included in the Book of Psalms. This chapter gives people an overview of the Book of Psalms and introduces some of the difficulties and some of the commonalities found throughout the Psalms.

Each of the four lessons on Psalms contains an option that will enable your class to create their own individual or communal psalms, modeled on the work of the original psalmists. If you plan to use this option on a regular basis, you might also want to arrange for class members to compile some type of booklet or scrapbook in which to keep their psalms. You might ask for a volunteer to be the editor or compiler of psalms for this project. (See option "G.") Be sure to allow people the option of not sharing any composition they wish to keep private.

If class members prove to be talented and interested in this kind of creative exercise, you might want to suggest that these psalms could be used in a devotional booklet to be shared with others in your congregation (perhaps with those whose health keeps them from coming to church on a regular basis). Or your class's psalms could be incorporated into your congregation's Sunday worship service.

The study of Psalms offers a wonderful opportunity to include music and the use of the hymnbook into your Sunday school class. If you do not feel comfortable leading singing, you may want to recruit a choir member or another musically talented person to help with opening worship for your class.

Keeping in mind the ways your class members learn best, as well as their needs and interests, choose at least one learning segment from each of the three Dimensions.

Dimension 1: What Does the Bible Say?

(A) Open the class session with worship.

- For this opening worship option you will need copies of *The United Methodist Hymnal*. A Psalter reading on Psalm 150 (No. 862) will go nicely with today's lesson. Try singing the responses.
- Another option would be to sing (or read the text if the hymn is unfamiliar and a musician is not available) Charles Wesley's hymn, "Praise the Lord Who Reigns Above" (*The United Methodist Hymnal*, 96). As you will note this hymn is based on Psalm 150.

(B) Discuss Dimension 1 questions in the study book.

- There are no right or wrong answers to these questions. Always invite discussion and encourage new ideas.
  1. We cannot determine exactly what the problem is that confronts the speaker in Psalm 6. However, class members should be able to identify some particular *clues* in the text. Use this time to encourage them not to guess or to speculate but to identify specific words and phrases that act as clues to the reality of the psalmist's situation.
  2. Again, ask people to cite particular verses that seem to them to point to the reversals that the speaker in Psalm 30 has experienced. It is hard to say whether the speaker refers several times to one major reversal in life or if the speaker is recalling a number of such reversals over a period of time.
  3. As the class members share their mental pictures of what was going on in the background as Psalm 47 was recited, encourage people to stick to the text as much as possible. (For example, What does the leader encourage people to do in verse 1?)
  4. Do not just count the different ways of praising the Lord in Psalm 150, encourage people to name them and to list them. It can become an actual act of praise to do this simple exercise.
     —To tie this activity into option "I," divide the chalkboard or a large piece of paper into three columns.
     —At the top of each column write one of the following headings: Ways of praising the Lord; Places for praising the Lord; Reasons for praising the Lord.
     —Under each heading list what you find in Psalm 150. Then save this list to use in option "I."

(C) Paraphrase the Psalms.

- Trying to restate in your own words what a psalmist has said is a sure way to test your comprehension of a psalm's content. Use either Psalm 6 or Psalm 30 for this exercise but not both.
- If your class is large enough, divide class members into as many small groups as there are verses in a psalm. (For Psalm 6, you will need ten groups, for Psalm 30 you will need twelve groups.)
- Assign a different verse to each group. For smaller classes, divide into five or six groups and assign two verses to each group. If your class is very small, assign a verse or two to each person.
- Then ask each group/person to reduce the parallel lines in their assigned verse or verses into a single statement that captures the essential thought-content of that verse.
- Give people five to ten minutes to compose and record their paraphrases, then share them aloud in numerical order (first verse 1, then verse 2, and so on).

Dimension 2: What Does the Bible Mean?

(D) Begin a psalm-line.

- As the study book points out, the Book of Psalms is not necessarily arranged in a logical pattern overall. However, there are some psalms that can be grouped together. These groupings are pointed out in "Hymn Book of Israel," page 31 of the study book.
- Using a roll of computer paper, banner paper, or a large posterboard, make a chart of the Psalms beginning with the groupings pointed out in the study book.
- Make a horizontal line along the middle of the banner or poster, with small vertical lines for the psalm numbers.
- Then, above the psalm-line, note the groupings mentioned in the study book by using brackets, or color bars with titles. For example, Psalms 73–83 could have a bracket above them, pointing to the words "Psalms of Asaph."
- The space below the psalm-line should be reserved for the notes of the class members as they go through their study of the Psalms. These notes could consist of the categories from option "B," or they could be made-up titles class members assign to certain psalms as they study them. (See "Sample Psalm-Line" on the inside back cover.)
- In addition, small pictures—either cut from magazines or drawn—could be placed below the psalm-line to reflect the students' feelings about particular psalms.
- This chart will resemble a timeline; but instead of dates, psalm numbers will be listed in order. Thus, it can be titled a "psalm-line."
- If you have the space in your classroom to do so, you could allot an inch to each Psalm from 1 to 150 and come out with a chart almost thirteen feet long! This would certainly give class members a good feel for the length of the Book of Psalms. However, the size of your chart can be scaled down by making a diagonal mark along the line for every five or ten Psalms, leaving room to simply note and highlight either the psalms that you study or those of particular interest to class members.
- If you can keep the psalm-line posted from week to week class members can add on whatever information they gain about the Psalms as they progress in their studies over the next few weeks. Use of such a psalm-line could help class members get a good overview of the Psalms. Further, it will show the class (and you, the teacher) what psalms have been studied more in-depth and those psalms that have been missed. The latter might make a good list of psalms for students to focus on in future classes or in their personal Bible study and devotional time.

SEASONS OF THE HEART AND SPIRIT

(E) Make posters to help in psalm identification.

- For this activity, you will need posterboard or large pieces of paper and markers.
- In the study book, at the top of page 32, there is a listing of some different types of Psalms: hymns, psalms of praise, psalms of confidence, psalms of lament, thanksgiving psalms, wisdom psalms, historical psalms, and royal psalms.
- Go over the descriptions of these types of psalms as given in the study book.
- Ask class members to make small posters containing these categories and a brief definition of each. Post these posters around the classroom and refer to them throughout your study of the Psalms.
- List each of the psalms studied today under the category you think fits it best.

(F) Explain the meaning of the term *Hallelujah*.

- Say: "Whether you know it or not, you all know an entire sentence in Hebrew. The term *hallelu* is the plural command form meaning 'Praise ye,' and *Yah* (or Jah) is a shortened form of the Hebrew name for God (*Yahweh*, translated LORD)." Look briefly at the psalms in which this term is used (see the last paragraph of the "Additional Bible Helps," page 22, for a listing).
- If your singing will not disturb others, do this: Ask if people know the game song "Praise Ye the Lord, Hallelujah." (If not, perhaps someone knows it well enough to teach it to others.) Sing it through twice, dividing the parts (first the men sing, "Praise ye the Lord," while the women respond, "Hallelujah"; then the women sing, "Praise ye the Lord," while the men respond, "Hallelujah"). If everyone in your class is able to stand up and sit down easily, you can have people stand as they sing their parts. Otherwise, ask people to raise their hands above their heads when they sing their assigned parts.

Dimension 3:
What Does the Bible Mean to Us?

(G) Become a modern-day psalmist: Write a psalm of praise.

- Give each class member paper, pencil, and time to work. Give the following directions:
—Think back to a time when you felt extremely happy, fortunate, lucky, or blessed. (Give people a moment to think).
—Remember who (or what) was there when you first shared or celebrated your good news (even if it was only grass and trees, or the four walls of a room).
—Now on your paper: Write a call to praise in which you call whatever or whomever was present with you at that time to help you offer praise to the God who made your joy possible. (Give people a minute or two to write this).
—Next, write some reasons why God should be praised concerning this particular occasion of joy. (Give people time to do this.)
—End your psalm with an echo or a repetition of the words you used to begin your call to praise.
- Before closing, allow time for class members to share their individual psalms with the rest of the class, *if they wish to do so*. If they have decided to compile a booklet of psalms (see "Learning Menu," page 18), give copies of those psalms to be collected to the designated collector or editor.
- Close this session with the psalm of a class member who is willing to share her or his writing as a prayer. The closing psalm could be read aloud by its author, or it could be passed around the class with each class member reading a different stanza. This choice should be made by the author of the closing psalm.

(H) Write a communal psalm of thanksgiving.

- Agree upon a communal experience. Ask class members to decide on a specific crisis that has happened in the church, in the community, or in the nation from which people may feel they have been saved by the Lord. Has the church or the community managed to survive or to rebuild itself after a flood, fire, drought, tornado, or the closing down of a major employer in the community?
—Begin with an address to God.
—Name or describe the experience.
—Express the community's thanks for God's role in helping them survive this experience.
—Have people recall and state how they felt while they were in the midst of this crisis. What did they say to God on that distressful occasion?
—How did God respond to their prayers?
—Conclude with a statement about how it feels to have been saved like this. Is it going to make any difference in how we act in the future?
- If you are going to keep and use this psalm for other purposes, be sure that all who have participated in this session are listed as co-authors.

(I) How can we praise you? Let us name the ways!

- Use the three lists begun in option "B." Ask class members to suggest other *Ways*, *Places*, and *Reasons* they have to praise the Lord (in addition to the ones listed in Psalm 150).
- If you have space, add another column and list *Who* (different categories of creatures that can praise the Lord—

animals, children, youth, the poor, the rich, and so on).
- To close, you might read the entire list as a psalm of praise.

(J) Make posters for "seasons of the heart and spirit."

- For this activity you will need four sheets of posterboard and other art supplies listed below.
- Focusing on the theme of this chapter, make a poster for each season of the year. You could either do this ahead of time, or split class members into four groups and let them make the posters. If you decide to have the class illustrate the posters themselves, you might provide them with such things as magazines, scissors, glue, and other art materials such as tissue paper (for making flowers and/or leaves), construction paper, markers, crayons, and so on. You might want to simply place these items on one central table in the room, and let the four groups get to creating.
- Use regular posterboard, placed so that it is tall rather than wide. Then split each posterboard into three sections by drawing two evenly spaced lines horizontally across the posterboard.
- The middle section will be used to illustrate the season by using the materials listed above. Leave the top and bottom sections blank for now.
- When the seasonal scenes are finished, put the posters up around the room. Ask class members to discuss what "seasons of the heart and spirit" might correspond to the different seasons of the year.
—Which of the psalms studied today fit best into which of the seasons? (This should be open to creative answers, as the point is not to make strict categories, but to air all the different feelings expressed in the Psalms.)
- Following this discussion, ask class members to do an "active" closing prayer.
- Give each class member a marker. Tell them they will be quietly adding to the season posters. This will involve looking through some of the psalms they have studied this week and choosing some passages that might be good descriptions of a particular season.
- Those passages should be either cited or copied onto the tops of their corresponding season posters.
- The bottom sections of the posters are to be used for class members' personal descriptions of these seasons of the heart and spirit.
- This time of "active prayer" can be completed as class members mill around the posters, read the verses and comments printed on them, and leave quietly.

(K) Practice walking in the shoes of the psalmists.

- Ahead of time: Make sure that a variety of different Bible translations (versions) are available in the classroom for comparative purposes. Try to find a *New English Bible*, a *Jerusalem Bible*, a New International Version, a New Revised Standard Version, and a King James Version of the Bible.
- Break class members into four groups, and assign each group one of the psalms focused on in this chapter (6, 30, 47, 150). Make sure that every group has at least two different translations of the Bible available to study.
- Write the following tasks where everyone can see them, and give the groups time to work:
—Read what the study book says about the psalm.
—Ask one person to read the psalm aloud to the group while others follow along in their Bibles.
—Compare the different translations of the psalm. Look for significant differences—differences that affect the meaning or your understanding of the psalm.
—Discuss: What is the overall mood or feeling-tone of this psalm?
—What do you think might have been going on in the life of the person who first composed this psalm at the time when it was composed?
—Why does the psalmist say what is said here? What is the motive that underlies this composition?
- When the groups have had sufficient time to complete their tasks, ask each group to report its findings to the rest of the class. If you have chosen to make a psalm-line, ask each group to write a few items of information or insights gained about their psalm in the area below the psalm-line.
- If you made posters to help with psalm identification, add what you have learned about the type of emotion that may accompany the types of psalms you have studied today (for example, on the psalm poster [option "E"] you might write "joy" or "exuberance").

Additional Bible Helps

The Use of the Psalms in the New Testament
The New Testament is filled with references to the Psalms. Jesus and the disciples sang psalms, and Paul quoted passages from the Psalms in his letters. The Gospel writers, as well as the authors of Ephesians and Hebrews, used the Psalms to illustrate their beliefs about who Jesus was and what he represented.

New Testament Christians believed they were living at the end of time and that a new age would soon come. They interpreted Scripture as a clue to God's activity in this crucial time in history. Some of the Psalms (and other Old Testament passages) were used by New Testament authors as proof texts, to make a theological point.

The Psalms were often used by New Testament authors to explain who Jesus was and the nature of the good news he preached. Christian writers believed that Old Testament texts pointed to Christian realities, applying the term "Son of Man" from Psalm 8 to Jesus, interpreting Jesus as the "stone that the builders rejected" from Psalm 118:22, and portraying Jesus as the king or as corporate Israel, so often mentioned in the Psalms.

Jesus himself used the Psalms in his teaching and prayers. We often forget that Jesus was Jewish. As a Jew, he would have known many of the Psalms by memory. He would have prayed the Psalms and recited them at Jewish feast days, such as the Passover. The story of the Last Supper, which is told as a celebration of the Passover, says, "When they had sung the hymn, they went out to the Mount of Olives" (Mark 14:26). At the Passover, Psalms 113–118 (called the "Hallel" in Jewish tradition) were sung in praise of God. The hymn to which Mark refers is most likely the Hallel.

The Sermon on the Mount contains many references to the Psalms. "Blessed are the meek, for they will inherit the earth" (Matthew 5:5) is reminiscent of Psalm 37:11. Matthew 5:34-35 contains a quotation from Psalm 48:3: "Mount Zion [Jerusalem] . . . the city of the great King." Matthew 6:26, "Look at the birds of the air; they neither sow nor reap, . . . yet your heavenly Father feeds them," and Luke 12:24, "Consider the ravens," come from Psalm 147:9, "He gives to the animals their food, / and to the young ravens when they cry." Jesus used the Psalms just as other Jewish rabbis used the Psalms, to teach listeners something about God.

Jesus also used the Psalms in his personal prayer. His prayers from the cross indicate that in his deepest distress, he prayed the Psalms. "My God, my God, why have you forsaken me?" is the beginning of a cry of lament from Psalm 22, recorded in Mark 15:34 and Matthew 27:46. "Father, into your hands I commend my spirit" (Luke 23:46) is a quotation from Psalm 31:5.

Paul, who was trained as a Jewish teacher, used the Psalms to claim that Jesus is the Messiah foretold in holy Scripture. Paul's words, "For he [Christ] must reign until he has put all his enemies under his feet. The last enemy to be destroyed is death. For 'God has put all things in subjection under his feet' " (1 Corinthians 15:25-27), allude to Psalm 110:1 and Psalm 8:6.

Paul used the psalms of lament for his own theological purposes. He used descriptions of the "wicked" in these psalms to mean those who have not accepted the gospel (compare Psalms 14:1-2, 53:1-2, 5:9, 140:3, and 10:7 to Romans 3:10-18 and Psalm 69:23-24 to Romans 11:9-10). Paul used the psalmists' descriptions of the suffering of the innocent to refer to the hardships faced by Christians (compare Psalm 44:22, "Because of you we are being killed all day long, / and accounted as sheep for the slaughter," to Romans 8:36; and compare Psalm 69:9b, "the insults of those who insult you have fallen on me," to Romans 15:3).

The Letter to the Hebrews makes heavy use of Old Testament Scriptures to prove that God has spoken to the present age through his Son, Jesus. For example, a quotation from one of the royal psalms makes the author's point that Jesus reigns with God as God's Son: "You are my Son; today I have begotten you" (Hebrews 1:5 and Psalm 2:7). Hebrews 1:8-9 ("Your throne, O God, is forever and ever, / and the righteous scepter is the scepter of your kingdom. / You have loved righteousness and hated wickedness; / therefore God, your God, has anointed you / with the oil of gladness beyond your companions") treats Jesus as the anointed one, the royal bridegroom, as in Psalm 45:6-7. (For more information about the royal psalms and their messianic interpretation, see the "Additional Bible Helps" in Chapter 5, page 27). The author of Hebrews casts Christ in the role of a new Moses, and in Hebrews 3–4 uses language from Psalm 95:8-11 to warn the Christians not to be like the rebellious Israelites wandering in the desert.

Our familiar shout of joy during Holy Week and Easter is a direct quotation from the Psalms, used in Revelation 19:1, 3, 4, and 6. *Hallelujah* is a Hebrew phrase, meaning "Praise the Lord!" It occurs at least twenty-three times from Psalm 104:35 through Psalm 150:6. Psalms 106, 113, 117, 135, and 146–150 begin and end with "Hallelujah." Psalms 111 and 112 begin with "Hallelujah," and Psalm 116 ends with "Hallelujah." In early Christian worship, saying "Hallelujah," or its Greek transliteration, "Alleluia," was associated with the reading or singing of the Gospel.

5 "Whom Have I in Heaven But You?"

Psalms 91; 44; 73

LEARNING MENU

As you continue in your study of the Book of Psalms, remember to continue any projects you started last week (such as writing psalms for a booklet, detailing a psalm-line, or adding to "seasonal" posters). Suggestions for using each of these with this week's lesson will be given below.

Remember that one of the points in studying the psalms is to connect with the emotions related by the psalmists. That may mean that your class members will be provoked to sadness, joy, and/or confusion right along with the psalmists. Be aware of this and be ready to be sensitive and flexible about it. Such emotions may occasionally dictate a last-minute change in teaching plans, which is fine.

Keeping in mind the ways your class members learn best, as well as their needs and interests, choose at least one learning segment from each of the three Dimensions.

Dimension 1: What Does the Bible Say?

(A) Hold an opening worship.

● A suggestion for your opening worship time is to sing together (or read the words to) the hymn "I'll Praise My Maker While I've Breath," *The United Methodist Hymnal*, 60. (More information on the history of this hymn is given in the study book, "A Wesley Favorite," page 44.)

(B) Answer the questions in the study book.

● Discussion of Dimension 1 questions might lead you in these directions:
  1. Answers given to the first question will probably focus on either a general idea of God's action toward the faithful, or on whole verses describing these things. To help class members take a fresh look at what this psalm says, divide a large piece of paper (or a section of your chalkboard) into two columns. At the top of one column put "nouns"; at the top of the other put "verbs." Ask class members to name first

the nouns and then the verbs that describe what the faithful can expect God to do for them (verbs) or to be for them (nouns). For example, the verb *deliver* could be mentioned (from 91:3) and the nouns *refuge* and *fortress* could be noted (from 91:2).

2. In order to get clear about what has happened that makes the speakers in Psalm 44 think God has been "asleep on the job," follow the same pattern as with question 1, listing nouns and verbs. If possible, keep the answers from question 1 in front of class members, since the second half of Psalm 44 will show extreme differences between itself and Psalm 91. The verb list for Psalm 44 should include *rejected* (verse 9) and *sold* (verse 12), while the noun list could include *taunt* (verse 13) and *laughingstock* (verse 14). All these examples are based on the New Revised Standard Version (NRSV). If you are using another translation you may find slightly different words to put in your lists.

3. In order to get people to discuss what they have gleaned from reading Psalm 73, ask leading questions:
   —Whom did the psalmist envy and why? (73:3-5)
   —What does the psalmist see happening to the wicked? (73:6, 10-12)
   —What keeps the psalmist from following in the footsteps of the wicked? (73:15)
   —What happened to persuade the psalmist that envy of the wicked was unnecessary? (73:16-20)

(C) Look for changes in speakers.

- Ask people to turn to Psalm 73 in their Bibles. Explain: A change in speakers can be indicated either by punctuation provided by the translators or by the sense of the words themselves. Quotation marks are added by the translators to give clues to readers about a change in speaker or voice. There are no such things as quotation marks in the original Hebrew.
- Ask people to read through Psalm 73, looking for the use of quotation marks. (Many translations will have them in verses 11 and 15.)
- Discuss: What do the quotation marks indicate to the reader? Who is it who says, "How can God know?" in verse 11?
- Next ask people to turn to Psalm 91. Ask them to imagine that they were going to make this psalm into a dramatic reading.
  —Then ask them, "Where would you end the first speaker's part and begin the second speaker's part?" and "Where would you have the third speaker begin to read?"
- If people seem to need help in order to make these decisions, tell them to look first for the use of quotation marks in their translations of this psalm. (Most versions use quotation marks in 91:2.) Ask, "What do these quotation marks mean?"
- Next have people look at Psalm 91:14-16. Some translations will have quotation marks here, and some will not.

Ask class members to say *who* they think is speaking here and *why* they think so.
- Ask people to turn to Psalm 44. Again ask where they would have the speakers change for a dramatic reading of this psalm. Be sure that people notice how the pronouns change from plural (we, our, us) in verse 1 to singular (my) in verse 4, and again in verses 5 (we) and 6 (my). Explain: Another way of telling when speakers change is by noting when the personal pronouns change from singular to plural.

Dimension 2: What Does the Bible Mean?

(D) Work on your psalm-line.

- If you began a psalm-line (Chapter 4, option "D"), add to it by labeling the psalms studied in this session. Remember, the space above the psalm-line is for indicating which psalms belong to larger groupings or collections. The section below the psalm-line can be used to label, categorize, or comment on specific psalms.
- Split class members into three groups, assigning each group a psalm from this week's lesson. Ask the groups to do the following:
—Note what the study book says about the psalm.
—Compare at least three different translations of the psalm, in order to point out problems and enhance understanding of the psalm's meaning.
—Decide what kind of psalm this is, using the types given and described in Chapter 4 of the study book (page 32). Does your psalm best fit into the category of hymns, psalms of praise, psalms of confidence, psalms of lament, thanksgiving psalms, wisdom psalms, historical psalms, or royal psalms?
—Try to think of your own original heading or title—a short phrase that describes what you think this psalm is all about.
- As each group finishes studying its psalm, ask someone from the group to function as a scribe and to write some of the significant information about it on the psalm-line, under the corresponding psalm number. Then ask the groups to give a brief report of their findings to the rest of the class.
- If you did not choose to make a psalm-line, this option could still be used by simply doing what is outlined above, leaving out the steps that involve the psalm-line.

(E) Identify the seasons of the heart in these psalms.

- Split class members into three groups, assigning each group one of this week's psalms—91, 44, or 73.
- Ask each group to make a list of all the different feelings mentioned in their psalm, making an effort to stick with

actual words contained in the psalm and noting verse references. Look for things in the psalm that could be picked up by the five senses: what are things in this psalm that could be smelled, touched, seen, tasted, or heard?
- When the groups have had sufficient time (five minutes or so should be enough), ask them to report their findings to the whole class.
- If you chose in the first week of your study of Psalms to make the "Seasons of the Heart and Spirit" posters, use these lists of emotions to help the group decide which psalm belongs to which "season." Ask for volunteers to list these new psalms on the appropriate posters.

(F) Examine the poetic language used in the psalms.

- Divide class members into three groups. Ask each group to look closely at Psalm 91:1-4 and to discuss:
—What two things are implicitly compared in verse 3? What is the implied image? How is the danger that threatens in verse 3 pictured?
—What is God implicitly compared to in the first two lines of verse 4? What picture do these lines call up in your mind? (You may need to supply people with a definition for the NRSV's "pinions," which is a word referrring to the flight feathers on a bird's wings.)
—What is the relationship between the image in verse 3 and the image in the first two lines of verse 4?
—What is God compared to in the last line of verse 4? How is this image like and how is it different from the image presented in the first two lines of this verse?
- When the groups have had time to come to some conclusions, ask for a delegate from each group to come to the front and make a rough sketch or drawing of the way God's protection is pictured in these verses. Stress that their efforts will not be judged for artistic merit! If you have a psalm-line or seasonal posters, the drawing could be done on one or the other of these as well.
- Discuss what each group discovered about the figurative language used in this psalm.

Dimension 3: What Does the Bible Mean to Us?

(G) Discuss the psalms and nonbiblical literature.

- From the discussion in the study book about psalms of orientation, disorientation, and new orientation ("The Flow of Human Life," page 42), ask class members to list examples of nonbiblical literature, popular songs, or movies that reflect similar attitudes.
- Start three lists on the board or on a large piece of paper. Label them "orientation," "disorientation," and "new orientation."
- Come to class time prepared with a list of well-known songs, movies, and so on that you think most class members will have heard or seen. (If you have a recording of one of your song examples, bring the recording to play in the session.) Name a song (for example) and ask people whether they think it expresses an attitude of orientation (confidence, sure expectations), disorientation (things are not working out the way the singer thought they would or should), or new orientation (a "survivor" looking back on a time of crisis and its resolution).
- Discuss: How are these examples from our culture like and how are they unlike the psalms? What is the primary area of difference?
- If your class time is at a closing point, you could play the song or read part of the words for a quiet closing worship time.

(H) Become a modern-day psalmist.

- Compose a communal lament (a psalm of communal disorientation) patterned after Psalm 44.
- On the board or on a large piece of paper, write the first line of Psalm 44. Then ask class members to list things they have heard other people say that God has done for them.
—Ask people to make a statement that summarizes what they believe about the nature of God. Write this on the board or on paper.
—Ask people to mention recent occasions when they have prayed for God's intervention or help and have not received it. List some of these.
—Ask people to list some of the questions they want to ask God about those occasions in which they did not get what they prayed for.
—Ask people to give reasons why they think God should respond favorably to them.
—End with Psalm 44:26 or a similar statement.
- Recruit a "scribe" to write your psalm in a finished form and to give it to your booklet editor (if the class has chosen to keep a collection of their creative work).
- Discuss: How do you feel about making such complaints to God? Is this an acceptable way for Christians to pray? Why do you think it is or is not a model that Christians can imitate in their own prayers?
- Close by reading your psalm out loud together.

(I) Decide which psalm best describes me today.

- Divide class members into three groups, choosing their group according to how they presently feel about their faith: oriented, disoriented, or verging on new orientation.

- Below are some guidelines for discussion appropriate to each of the three groups. Since you cannot be in all three groups, write some of these suggestions on index cards or pieces of paper and give them to the groups for their guidance.
- All the groups should begin by reading together their corresponding psalm (Psalm 91=orientation; Psalm 44=disorientation; Psalm 73=new orientation). This reading can take a number of different forms in order to help the group really hear and understand the feelings of the psalmist. For example, one person can read the psalm out loud to the group, the whole group can read the psalm together, the group can read the psalm by taking turns reading a stanza, or group members can take turns reading sections (like paragraphs) of the psalm.
- *The Orientation Group* (Psalm 91) should first focus on how the psalmist feels about God:

—Are there reasons given to explain why the psalmist trusts in God?

—What does this trust mean for the psalmist?

Then the group should discuss what it means for them to have such sure faith in God.

—What kinds of qualities do they attribute to God?

—Are there any drawbacks or pitfalls that can come along with such sure faith? (Take a moment here to read Luke 4:9-12.)

—Have there been times when your feelings of orientation/confidence in God's protection have been threatened by real-life experiences?

—What is it like to move out of such an "oriented" feeling of faith? Why does this happen or what causes it? What happens next?

- *The Disorientation Group* (Psalm 44) should begin by considering such questions as:

—What is the main point being made by the speakers in Psalm 44?

—What feelings are being expressed in this psalm?

—What is this psalmist's dilemma?

From there, the group should move into some more personal questions:

—Have you ever had similar feelings or felt the same way the speakers in Psalm 44 feel?

—How does it make you feel to know such protest is contained in Scripture?

—How easy or how hard is it for you to voice your feelings honestly to God?

—When protesting to God, are you able to be direct, or do you hide your feelings in pious language?

—Do you feel guilt at protesting to God? If so, how can the presence of such psalms as this one help you deal with that guilt?

—What struggles might you be having right now (which you are comfortable sharing) which you have been putting forth to God, or would like to be presenting to God?

—What would be your final demand of God today, if you felt free to offer your ultimate protest?

—How does one begin to move out of disorientation?

- *The New Orientation Group* (Psalm 73) should first get clear about the following:

—What was it that had caused the speaker in Psalm 73 to experience some disorientation in the past? What expectations had the psalmist had that were not fulfilled?

—What was the turning point that led the psalmist to a new orientation?

—What was the content of this new orientation? What new thoughts, beliefs, or expectations does the speaker come to have at the end of Psalm 73?

Then members of this group can begin to discuss:

—What religious beliefs or expectations have you had that did not seem to hold true to your real-life experiences?

—How did you react, or how did this discrepancy between belief and experience make you feel?

—What new orientation, new beliefs, or expectations do you know that have replaced the old ones?

—How was this change accomplished for you?

—What made it possible for you to attain a new orientation?

—How do you think God was involved in that process?

—Do you think God was involved in the stages before and after that process took place?

- Ask each group to have its own closing prayer, in which each group member is offered a chance to say a few words based on their discussion.

(J) Close with a psalm reading.

The Twenty-third Psalm is perhaps the most familiar of all the Psalms. Its impact on individual and corporate spiritual life is deep and rich. This psalm is classified as a psalm of confidence, a psalm of new orientation.

The opening sentence is a metaphor—"The LORD is my shepherd." When we speak these words we profess God's provision and care of us, our total dependence on God.

This psalm confirms God's companionship with us. Yes, evil is in the world, but God continues to be with us "all the days of my [our] life."

- Ask class members to close their eyes and to sit comfortably. *Do not tell them the closing worship time will be based on the Twenty-third Psalm.* Say something like this: "Try to free your mind of other thoughts. Let the morning's concerns fade away, know that family demands can wait. Be ready to allow ancient biblical words to enter your mind and heart." Wait a few quiet moments . . . then begin to read the psalm slowly. At the end of the reading allow a few more quiet moments.
- Close with a prayer that thanks God for these important words of comfort. You could allow class members to share how this psalm has strengthened them over the years.

Additional Bible Helps

Royal Psalms and Messianic Expectations

As the people of God moved into the Promised Land, it was the Lord who was first considered King in Israel (Judges 8:23). Some of the historians of Israel saw the people's initial demand for an earthly king as a rejection of the sovereignty of God in the land (1 Samuel 8:7). Others believed that David and the kings of the Davidic line were God's designated representatives, delegated by God to carry out God's will in the land of Judah through their reigns. In this capacity, the kings were referred to as the servants of God and as the "sons" of God (see 2 Samuel 7:14a and Psalm 89).

Psalm 2 seems to have originated as a royal psalm. It was first meant to be a psalm that a newly crowned king of Judah could recite at his own enthronement ceremony. Vassal nations are warned not to revolt at this time when the crown is passing from father to son (2:1-3), because God has guaranteed the succession (2:4-6). In 2:7-9 the new king quotes God's words to him; and then he addresses other rulers, warning them to serve the Lord in order to avoid bringing about their own destruction.

The statement that the king has become the "son" of God (Psalm 2:7) was a common feature in ancient coronation rites (see 2 Samuel 7:14a and 1 Chronicles 22:10; 28:6). But the New Testament community understood these references to God's "son" as references to the divine sonship of Jesus.

Kings of Judah were "anointed" or rubbed with oil as a sign of the Lord's approval of their right to govern the land. The kings' throne in Jerusalem was called the "throne of the LORD" (1 Chronicles 29:23). The words that mean "to anoint" or "to rub with oil" are the words *messiah* in Hebrew and *christos* in Greek. Thus when Hebrew speakers refer to "the Messiah" or when Greek speakers refer to "the Christ," they are referring to "the Anointed One."

Christians are accustomed to speaking of only one Messiah (Jesus is said to be "the Christ" or "the Anointed One" of God). But in ancient Israel, the title *messiah* or *anointed one* was applied to a variety of different people. For most of Israel's history, the term *messiah* or *anointed one* was applied to earthly kings (and occasionally to priests). The "anointed of the LORD" were supposed to be people of power commissioned to carry out God's will in their earthly spheres of influence. Thus Isaiah 45:1 says that Cyrus, the Persian who freed the people of Judah from their exile in Babylon is God's anointed (literally, the "messiah" or the "christ" of the Lord).

While the kings of Judah were expected to oversee peace, justice, and righteousness in the land, to defend the defenseless and crush the oppressor (Psalm 72), David's descendants seldom lived up to the people's (or to God's) expectations. Those who expected (or at least hoped) that these ideals would be carried out by the earthly kings of Judah were regularly disappointed. This continual disappointment with the reality of earthly kingship seems to have led to a gradual shifting of people's expectations. Instead of hoping that one of their earthly kings would live up to his calling to be "a messiah," some people began to look forward to the coming of "*the* messiah"—an ideal, otherworldly figure who really would carry out God's will for justice and righteousness in the land.

Toward the end of the Old Testament period, sometime in between the Babylonian Exile and the birth of Jesus, the term *Messiah* also began to be applied to a divine figure whose coming was associated with the end of the world as we now know it. Even in New Testament times the people of Judah were divided in their expectations. Some people expected Jesus to rule like an ideal king on earth and others expected him to bring about the end of the unjust order of the world altogether.

Because of these overlapping terms and expectations, the royal psalms (which were originally written to, for, and about earthly kings) have often been read in Christian circles as statements pertaining to Jesus Christ. Thus, for instance, we can see that Psalm 45 was originally written to celebrate the occasion of a royal wedding between an earthly king and his earthly bride. The heading calls this psalm "a love song." The singer describes the luxurious trappings of the bride and her attendants in the wedding procession (45:8-9, 13-15) and offers the bride a bit of advice on how she should behave toward her husband (45:10-12). In the Hebrew, 45:6 reads, "Your throne is a throne of God, enduring forever," implying that the ruler who is getting married here has God's support and approval (see the parallel in 1 Chronicles 29:23).

In 45:7, the king whose wedding is celebrated here is said to have been "anointed" by God, as were all of the kings of David's line. But in the Septuagint (an early Greek translation of the Old Testament) the word *anointed* is translated by the Greek word *Christos* and the Greek translation seems to imply that the king himself was divine ("Your throne, O God, endures forever and ever"). It is the Greek text that is quoted in Hebrews 1:8-9. Thus the Greek version of Psalm 45:6-7 facilitated the early church's "messianic" reading of this text.

6
Psalms 58; 103; 113; 130

With the Lord There Is Steadfast Love

LEARNING MENU

As part of your planning for this session, read or review the article on "Popular Theology in Wisdom Literature and Psalms" (page 70) and the "Additional Bible Helps" section on "Forgiveness of Sins in the Psalms" (page 31).

The Psalms studied in this lesson present us with a variety of viewpoints on the nature of God and how God works in and with human lives. You will need to help class members see that not only do different people think differently about God, but we all think differently about God depending on our circumstances.

This lesson will also provide further opportunity to explore the figurative language of the Psalms, giving people additional chances to appreciate their literary beauty as well as their theological variety.

Remember to continue (or to add to) any projects that were started in previous sessions on the Psalms (such as a devotional booklet of original psalms, a psalm-line, or seasonal psalm posters).

Keeping in mind the ways your class members learn best, as well as their needs and interests, choose at least one learning segment from each of the three Dimensions.

Dimension 1: What Does the Bible Say?

(A) Open the session with worship.

- For this opening worship option you will need copies of *The United Methodist Hymnal*. A Psalter reading that goes nicely with today's lesson is Psalm 113 (No. 834). Try singing the responses.

(B) Answer the questions in the study book.

- Discussion of Dimension 1 questions might lead you in these directions.
  1. Encourage people to stick as closely as possible to the text of Psalm 58 when they discuss what this speaker wants God to do and why. There will be time later to discuss such issues as the justice of God.
  2. List on the chalkboard or on a large piece of paper the actual words that describe what people see to be God's most prominent characteristics in Psalm 103. You may want to save this list to use as a basis for further discussion in Dimension 2. It will be interest-

ing at this point also to reflect on some of the differences in mood between Psalms 103 and 58.

Also while discussing Psalm 103, make sure the class has recognized the "envelope structure" in it. This is the repetition of phrases that appear in the beginning of the psalm and at the end of the psalm. In this way, a sort of literary "envelope" surrounds the psalm and holds it together. In Psalm 103 the envelope structure is characterized by the phrase "Bless the LORD, O my soul" (NRSV) in verses 1 and 2 and repeated in verses 21 and 22.

3. It takes a while for the speaker in Psalm 113 to get around to mentioning what God has done, but verses 7-9 are fairly specific. Also in discussing this psalm, ask class members to identify its envelope structure, found in verses 1 and 9 in the phrase "Praise the LORD."

4. On the chalkboard or on a large piece of paper make a list of the qualities of God named by the speaker in Psalm 130 before you discuss which ones give the speaker hope. Again, you may want to save this list to use as a basis for further discussion in Dimension 2.

(C) Look at the verbal pictures in the Psalms.

- For this option you will need paper and markers or crayons.
- To add some visual interest to this exercise, look through magazines or books before this session and bring pictures of a poisonous serpent and/or an adder, a lion with its fangs bared, and a snail to class.
- Look at the metaphors that are used in Psalm 58.
—What picture do you get of the wicked? (What are the wicked said to be like in 58:4-5?)
—What would the wicked be like if the psalmist's prayers for revenge were answered (58:6-10)?
- Ask people to turn to Psalm 58. Hold up the pictures you collected, one by one, letting people identify and read aloud the appropriate verses in which the pictures are found.
- Turn to Psalm 113 and ask people to describe or draw the picture they get of God from this psalm. In this picture, where is God and where are we? What is God doing?
- Ask class members to draw the way human beings are pictured in Psalm 103. (They are like dust, verse 14; like grass and flowers in a dry wind, verses 15-16.)
- Discuss:
—What picture do you get of God from 103:19-22?
—How do you picture the beings that are called on to "Bless the LORD"?

Dimension 2:
What Does the Bible Mean?

(D) Look more closely at forgiveness of sins in the Psalms.

- Read the "Additional Bible Helps" material on this topic at the end of this leader's guide lesson and prepare to present substantial parts of the information it contains to your class.
- Ask people to look closely at Psalm 103:8 and 17-18 while you read (or a class member reads) Exodus 34:6 and Exodus 20:6 out loud. Ask persons to discuss:
—How do the Exodus passages differ from the Psalm 103 passages we just read?
—What might account for these differences?
—Which part of the Exodus 34:6 statement would the speaker in Psalm 58 have been most likely to emphasize?
—Why do you think the speakers in Psalm 58 and Psalm 103 emphasize different parts of the Exodus statement?
—What might have made this particular psalmist emphasize the forgiving side of God?
- Share some of the information from the "Additional Bible Helps" article concerning the various terms that are used for offenses against God and the slightly different shades of meaning each word has (iniquity in 103:3; sins in 103:10; and transgressions in 103:12). Read or summarize the information about forgiveness and the various picturesque terms the Old Testament authors use to describe forgiveness.
- If you choose this option, follow your presentation on "forgiveness" with the discussion in option "G."

(E) Picture the Lord of the psalmists.

Each psalmist has a somewhat different understanding of who the Lord is and what the Lord is like. Many of the descriptions of the Lord in these psalms are anthropomorphic, meaning that they assign human-like qualities to the Lord. For example, Psalm 103:19 refers to the Lord's "throne" (NRSV), which assumes both that the Lord has the human-like need to sit down somewhere and that the Lord has the human-like characteristics of a king.

The following exercise will encourage class members to look critically at the human-like roles the psalmists have assigned to God.

- Divide into three groups and assign one of these psalms to each group: 103, 113, 130.
- Ask each group to make a "verbal mug shot" of the Lord. Explain that the group is to give a detailed descrip-

tion of the Lord, one that comes out of the psalm on which the group is supposed to focus. Such a "verbal mug shot" might be compared to the introduction a guest speaker is given before taking the podium, to a resumé that tries to "sell" someone to a new employer, or to a caricature (like a political cartoon).

- If you have anyone with artistic talent in your group, you might encourage that person to draw caricatures based on these psalms.
- This exercise asks people to exaggerate the anthropomorphic features that already exist in the Psalms, just as caricatures, introductions, or resumés exaggerate or highlight certain features of the people they portray.
- Begin by sharing this example with class members: In Psalm 58, the Lord is compared with a judge (58:11). Imagine Psalm 58 portrayed in a modern courtroom. Ask yourself:

—If I could draw a caricature showing God as Judge, what would I show God wearing? (Possible answers might include: a black robe, maybe a wig like judges wear in an English court.)
—Where would I show God sitting? (behind a legal bench?)
—What would I put in God's hand? (a gavel?)
—What would I have God saying and to whom? (handing down what sort of sentence on the wicked?)
—What kind of expression would I put on God's face in my picture?
—What do I picture the righteous doing as the judge is handing down this verdict?

- When the groups have finished with their "verbal mug shots" or caricatures of the Lord as described in these three psalms, give them time to share their results with the rest of the class.
- Discuss with the whole class:

—What are the advantages and the drawbacks associated with describing God according to human roles or offices?

- If no one raised the issue in the above discussion, ask people to consider:

—What kind of picture is suggested by Psalm 103:13 (which compares God to a human father)? What are the advantages and disadvantages associated with picturing God as a human father?

(F) Work on your psalm-line.

- If your class members have been working on a psalm-line, there are a number of places in the study book that identify groupings that should be noted on the psalm-line. Remember, groupings of similar psalms are to be noted above the psalm-line, while notes about individual psalms are to be noted below it.
- Ask people to suggest items that should be noted on the psalm-line either from today's reading in the study book or from their personal examination of the psalms. You might suggest the following, if no one else does:

—"Do Not Destroy" is in the heading of Psalms 57–59 and Psalm 75. Before simply noting this grouping on the psalm-line, make sure the class notes what the study book said about this heading in regard to its possible meanings (page 48).
—"A Song of Ascents" (NRSV) is the heading assigned to Psalms 120–134. Again, make sure the class has noted what the study book says about the meaning of this title and its obscurity (page 49).

- In addition to noting these groupings, ask class members to get in pairs and come up with descriptive comments about each of this chapter's psalms to note below the psalm-line.

Dimension 3: What Does the Bible Mean to Us?

(G) Explore forgiveness for ourselves.

- To follow up on option "D," ask people to reread Psalm 58 and to try to put themselves in the "shoes" of the psalmist. Discuss:

—What emotion dominates Psalm 58?
—What seems to have caused the psalmist to feel this way?

- Turn to the person on your left (or right). Share with each other a time or a situation in which you have wished, hoped, or prayed for the Lord to punish sinners in a dramatic or graphic manner.
- Come back into the whole group, and discuss:

—Would it ever be appropriate for Christians to read or pray Psalm 58?
—If so, when or under what circumstances?
—Do you see a conflict between the way the psalmists spoke about their own enemies and the way they hoped for forgiveness from God?
—Can we expect God to forgive us for our sins even when we are not willing to forgive others?

- To close, read Psalm 51:1-12.

(H) Work on seasons posters.

One of the things that may have become apparent to class members in studying this week's psalms is that what we think about the Lord and what we want from the Lord grow out of the current "seasons" of our hearts and spirits.

- If your class began the "Seasons of the Heart and Spirit" posters in Chapter 4, here is another chance to add to them. (Of course, if you did not begin them then and would like to now, that is certainly possible! See option "J" in Chapter 4 of this leader's guide for guidance [page 21].)
- Begin this process by dividing class members into four

groups. Each group will focus on one of the psalms from this chapter (58, 103, 113, or 130).
- Each group's task is to discern what "seasons" of the heart and spirit are mentioned in its psalm and to determine what season of the year it thinks corresponds to the season of the psalm.
— Each group should come up with both specific references and general moods from the psalms. For example, a group might decide that Psalm 58 has a tone of bitterness and vengeance and thus could correspond to the bitter cold of winter. Or a group might think that Psalm 103:5 (which seems to describe God's abundance and the psalmist's keen awareness of such) should go on the fall poster, since fall is a time we associate with the abundance of the harvest.
- After the groups are finished ask a spokesperson from each group to share its reasoning and add its psalm to the appropriate poster. Give people in other groups time to respond, to agree or disagree with the choices others have made. There will be disagreements, but the goal of this exercise is to air all the different feelings expressed in the psalms and to see how they relate to our own.

(I) Become a modern-day psalmist.

Option One:
One way to make a psalm into your own prayer is through an interpretive paraphrase, which tries to "update" the problems and the petitions of the original psalm without losing the essence of the original.
- Ask class members to look closely at Psalm 113. Note that "Praise [of] the LORD" (verses 1, 9) in this psalm is motivated by some very specific actions on God's part (in verses 7-9). Ask people to suggest answers to the following questions and to write their answers so all can see them:
— What is it that made barrenness a particular problem in the psalmist's world?
— What causes a similar problem for people in our world?
— What is it that all of the people who are said to be helped by "the LORD" in Psalm 113 have in common?
— Who in our own society would fit into the same category of need as those mentioned by the psalmist?
— Who in our local church or in our community has needs similar to those mentioned by the psalmist?
— Name some specific individuals or groups of people today whose rescue by the Lord would be a cause for praise.
- Now decide which of these statements you want to include in your updated paraphrase of this psalm. Close by asking someone to read your new version of Psalm 113 out loud, substituting your paraphrase for verses 7-9.

Option Two:
Some psalms are addressed directly to God and others are not. People who feel awkward or uncomfortable trying to compose their own psalms can be encouraged to personalize a biblical psalm by changing statements that talk in the third person *about* God into prayers that are addressed directly *to* God. For instance, using Psalm 150 as a model, we can say "I praise you O LORD. / I praise you in your sanctuary; / I praise you in your mighty firmament" and so on. This transformation has the additional advantage of making the language of the psalms less masculine and more universally acceptable to all who wish to pray them.
- If you choose this option, divide class members into two groups. One group can transform Psalm 113 and the other group can transform Psalm 103 into personal prayers (using changes such as "Who is like you, O LORD?" or "you raise the poor from the dust" in Psalm 113 and "You forgive all our iniquities, / you heal all our diseases" in Psalm 103).
- Ask a spokesperson from each group to read the finished product to the other half of the class, and allow these readings to stand as your closing prayers for this session.
- If you choose to do any of these options involving psalm composition or transformation, arrange for someone to record your creative efforts. If you are keeping a booklet or a scrapbook of Psalms, be sure to list all the participants as "authors" in this endeavor.

Additional Bible Helps

Forgiveness of Sins in the Psalms

A number of different Hebrew words are used to express the concepts of *sin* and *forgiveness* in the Psalms.

English translations have a difficult time finding enough synonyms for *sin* to translate all the Hebrew words with this meaning. For the most part, the NRSV translates the Hebrew word *hatta'ah* (meaning to miss the mark or to go wrong) as "sin" (as in Psalm 103:10). The word *pesha'* (with the basic sense of rebellion) is usually translated "transgression" (as in Psalm 103:12) and the word *'awon* is either translated "iniquity" (as in Psalm 103:3) or "guilt" (as in Psalm 51:5). An English reader can see that all these words are used as synonyms for offenses against God in Psalm 51:1-3. But the psalmists also use a variety of other phrases to describe wrongdoing, such as "doing what is evil in God's sight" (Psalm 51:4) or "rebelling against God" (Psalm 78:40).

In a similar way, Hebrew speakers use a variety of words and phrases to express the concept of *forgiveness*. One Hebrew word specifically means to be forgiven or to be pardoned by God, but this word is used only a few times in the Psalms (see Psalms 25:11; 103:3; 130:4). Most of the other words that represent the concept of forgiveness in the Psalms are less general and more graphic in their basic meanings. For instance, in Psalm 32, the word translated "forgiven/forgave" has the basic sense of *being lifted away*. The psalmist says, literally, "Happy are those whose transgression is *lifted away*, / whose sin is *covered*" (in 32:1) and "you *lifted away* the guilt of my sin" (in 32:5) (italics added).

In Psalm 78:38 the English word "forgave" translates a Hebrew word with the basic sense of *covered over* and in Psalm 130:4 the English "forgiveness" translates a Hebrew word meaning *sending away*. Psalm 130:8 says that God will "redeem" Israel from all its iniquities (using a word meaning "to ransom" captives). One psalmist asks God to "*blot out* my transgressions" (Psalm 51:1, italics added), while another rejoices because God "*removes* our transgressions from us" (Psalm 103:12, italics added). Thus many different words can be used to express the concept of forgiveness.

Psalm 103 is a good example of a psalm that is dedicated to praising God's forgiving nature. The psalmist begins his list of God's qualities with the term that refers to divine pardon in general. God is the one "who forgives all your iniquity" (103:3). The psalmist gives at least two reasons why it makes sense to believe that God "does not deal with us according to our sins, / nor repay us according to our iniquities" (103:10). The first reason has to do with God's nature. God is first of all "merciful and gracious . . . abounding in steadfast love" (103:8) and compassionate like a parent with a child (103:13). The second reason has to do with our own nature. God is forgiving because God remembers "how we were made" (103:14). As human beings, we know that none of us could survive if God actually punished all of our wrongdoings (Psalm 130:3). God knows this about us as well. The speaker in Psalm 78 gives the same reason to explain why God repeatedly forgave the people of Israel when they rebelled in the wilderness: "He remembered that they were but flesh, / a wind that passes and does not come again" (78:39).

Forgiveness is something the psalmists frequently ask for and hope for from God. However, very little (if anything) is said in the Psalms about forgiving one's enemies. The identity of the "enemies" in the Psalms varies from speaker to speaker. They are the "wicked," the wrongdoers, the mockers of God (Psalm 73). They can be described in natural or supernatural, social, political, or religious terms. When an entire community complains of defeat or oppression we usually think of Israel's national enemies. But enemies may also persecute or attack a psalmist personally, like criminals (Psalm 10), or as false witnesses in lawsuits (27:12; 35:11). Enemies may be those who take advantage of a person's illness or weakness (Psalm 38) or those who have betrayed a friend (Psalm 41). The enemy might be considered death itself (41:11) or someone who is eagerly waiting for the psalmist to die (41:5). Enemies may pose a threat to the health of an individual (as in Psalm 6) or to the survival of an entire nation (as in Psalms 44 or 79).

In any case, the psalmists are much more likely to ask God to punish their enemies than to forgive them. Modern readers are sometimes shocked when they discover that a number of psalms contain vicious petitions asking God to do all sorts of horrible things to the psalmists' enemies, who are often considered to be God's enemies as well. As we read these psalms (Psalms 5; 31; 35; 40; 55; 58; 79; 83; 137; 140) we need to remember that the psalmists expected retribution for sins to take place in this life. They expected God to punish and reward people according to their deeds (Psalm 62:12) in this life, in a fully visible manner (Psalm 58:10-11). They expected God to avenge the wrongs their enemies had done to them. Significantly, there is no evidence whatsoever that any of the psalmists tried to take vengeance into their own hands. The psalmists seem to have gained a degree of inner peace simply by handing their desire for vengeance over to God.

7
Psalms 13; 18:1-19; 22; 88

"My God, My God, Why Have You Forsaken Me?"

LEARNING MENU

While lament has long been an integral, important, valuable part of both the Jewish and the Christian traditions, popular piety teaches us to suppress (or be ashamed of) our feelings of grief and despair. Thus you may find that some of your students will be shocked to discover that a prayer of deep despair like Psalm 88 has been preserved in the canon. Others will feel a certain degree of liberation or comfort in the discovery that their hidden, innermost feelings have found expression in this biblical text. Make it clear that both responses (feelings of shock and feelings of liberation) are acceptable in God's presence.

Keeping in mind the ways your class members learn best, as well as their needs and interests, choose at least one learning segment from each of the three Dimensions.

Dimension 1:
What Does the Bible Say?

(A) Open with a time of worship.

- Here are three ideas for opening worship for this session.
  1. Play recorded chants or psalms. Gregorian chants seem to be timeless. (*Chant*, recorded by the monks of Domingo De Silos, is readily accessible. Angel Records, 1994.)
  2. Play "On the Willows" from *Godspell*; recorded by Bell Records, a Division of Columbia Pictures Industries, Inc.
  3. Read Psalter selection No. 752 in *The United Methodist Hymnal*. This reading is based on Psalm 22 and is often used for Good Friday.

(B) Answer the Dimension 1 questions in the study book.

- Discussion of the Dimension 1 questions may lead in these directions:
  1. As persons give their answers to this question, point out that the speaker in Psalm 13 is *petitioning* God, asking for God's help/deliverance.
  2. Along with class members' answers to this question, you may want to refer to the "Additional Bible Helps" article on "Theophany" (page 36), or save this information for option "E."
  3. The question about Psalm 22 is intended to get people to read the ending of the psalm with some care. If people had difficulty answering this question, point them toward verses 27-31.
  4. Ask people to cite the verses from which they have drawn their conclusions in order to answer this ques-

tion. The many possible answers that could be given to this question include such things as: God is a God of salvation (88:1); God is angry with the psalmist (88:7, 16); God has abandoned the psalmist (88:14); God has done all these things to the psalmist (88:6-8, 18); God does not work wonders for the dead (88:10).

(C) Compare the psalms in this lesson.

- Discuss with your class some of the following questions:
—What do Psalms 13, 22, and 88 have in common? (At the very least, people should notice that they are all laments, by people who feel abandoned by God and who want God to come to their rescue.)
—How is Psalm 88 different from Psalms 13 and 22? (One essential difference is the fact that Psalm 88 never moves toward a statement of confidence. The speaker in 88 seems caught up in despair, while the speakers in both 13 and 22 express confidence in God's favorable response to their pleas.)
—How does the perspective of the speaker in Psalm 18:1-19 differ from the perspective of the other speakers in Psalms 13, 22, 88? (The speaker in Psalm 18:1-19 is looking back on a past situation from which he has already been rescued.)

Dimension 2: What Does the Bible Mean?

(D) Picture this.

- For this activity you will need three pieces of posterboard or large pieces of paper, markers, pencils, and Bibles.
- Divide class members into three groups.
- Tell each group to read over the verses assigned to it and decide on how the dominant images in these assigned verses might be pictured on paper. Each group should appoint one of its members to draw these basic pictures on posterboard or paper. Stress that artistic talent is not needed for this exercise. Simple outlines that suggest the picture are adequate.

Part One—Psalm 18:1-19:
Assign Group 1 to study the way God is pictured in Psalm 18:1-3, Group 2 to study the way the danger that confronted the psalmist is pictured in 18:4-5, and Group 3 to study how the way God comes to the psalmist's rescue is pictured in 18:6-15.

Part Two—Psalm 22:
Assign 22:6-12 to Group 1, 22:13-16 to Group 2, and 22:19-21 to Group 3. Ask each group to try to picture the danger that threatens the psalmist in its assigned verses.

Ask people to remember that although Jesus quoted the first line of this psalm as he hung from the cross, someone else composed the psalm. They are trying to picture the danger faced by the original speaker.

- Then call class members back together and discuss the difference between literal and figurative language used in the Psalms.
—What is meant by the term *figurative language*? What is meant by *literal language*?
—How do you decide if something is to be understood literally or figuratively?
—Which of the pictures we have derived from Psalm 18 do you take to be figurative descriptions? Why do you think so?
—Are there any literal descriptions to be found in Psalm 18:1-19? If so, what are they?
—What kind of danger might the pictures we have derived from Psalm 22 point toward?

(E) Examine the psalmists' worldviews.

The term *worldview* refers to the assumptions people ordinarily make about how the world they live in is structured, what it looks like, how it works, and so on. Worldviews change dramatically as we move from ancient, prescientific cultures into our own time. The image we have of the earth as a blue and white globe (derived from pictures taken in space, looking down on the planet from a great height) is far different from the image of the earth ancient Israelites carried in their minds. In a similar way, modern peoples have developed views about life after death that vary greatly from the assumptions made by the psalmists.

- Before the session begins, read or review the material in the article "Popular Theology in Wisdom Literature and Psalms," page 70, and the information on "Theophany" in the "Additional Bible Helps," page 36. If you choose this option, a good follow-up to this discussion is option "H."
- Discuss: What is Sheol?
- Ask people to look at Psalm 18:4-5. On the chalkboard or on a large piece of paper, line up the parallel terms (the terms that are synonymous with each other in the thought rhyme):
- Using the NRSV, your parallels will look like this:

cords	death	encompassed me
torrents	perdition	assailed me
cords	Sheol	entangled me
snares	death	confronted me

(Other translations may use slightly different words.)

- Ask people what ideas are most closely thought-rhymed with *Sheol* in this verse. (*Sheol* and *death* are equated.)
- Now turn to Psalm 88 and look at 88:3-7 and 88:10-12. Read these verses out loud. Ask people to discuss: What picture do you get of Sheol and death from these

verses? (Notice words like *no help* or *forsaken* or *land of forgetfulness*.) What does this psalmist think will be the relationship between God and the dead?
- Share whatever further information you have gained from the "Additional Bible Helps" that you think is relevant to this discussion.
- Then discuss: What is all that storm imagery doing in Psalm 18?
- Reread Psalm 18:6-15 aloud, stopping at the end of every verse to discuss briefly what the words in that verse imply about God. What kind of picture is being drawn here of God's appearance?
- Write the word *theophany* on the board and explain its meaning (from the "Additional Bible Helps," page 36). Explain what kinds of things are often said to accompany a *theophany* in the Old Testament.
- Ask: Why do you think Old Testament people might have associated the appearance of God with the coming of a thunderstorm?

Dimension 3: What Does the Bible Mean to Us?

(F) Become a modern-day psalmist.

- By writing an individual psalm of lament, class members can get a full sense of the role the psalms played in the faith life of the individuals in ancient Israel.
- If you have not already done so, briefly review what the typical parts of a psalm of lament are, using the study book (page 56) and Psalm 13 as your example. Point out that a lament begins with an address to God, such as the phrase "O LORD" in Psalm 13:1. The address to God is usually followed by a statement of complaint, which describes the misery being felt or the danger being faced by the psalmist. The complaint can contain questions addressed to God about God's failure to respond and petitions requesting God to change the lamenter's present situation. Petitions are often connected to a rationale or a reason why this petition should be granted by the Lord. A petition may or may not be followed by a stanza of explanation.
- Note Psalm 13:5, in which the psalm of lament takes a marked turn in mood. Class members might want to make the latter half of their psalm change in such a way, but it is also possible to alternate statements of confidence and praise with petitions and complaints.
- Hand out paper, pens or pencils, and give people plenty of time and space to do this exercise.
- Write the following elements on the chalkboard or on a large piece of paper as a guideline for class members' compositions:

—Address (speak to) God or name God in some way.
—State a problem or a pain or a grief you feel.
—Ask God to do something very specific to change this situation.
—State why you think God should do what you have asked.
—Close with a statement of confidence in God's ability or willingness to help you.

- Before people begin to write, ask them to close their eyes for a moment. Tell them this: "Think about a time in which you have felt forsaken by God, or think about why you feel that way right now. Ask yourself how did I feel/do I feel when I was/am confronted by illness, death, alienation, oppression, depression, rejection, loss of job, natural disaster, betrayal by someone I trusted, failure to acheive my goals. Now write a personal prayer letter to God, keeping the above guidelines in mind as you write."
- Before your closing, allow time for class members to share their individual psalms with the rest of the class, *if they wish to do so*. If class members have decided to compile a booklet of psalms, let those who are interested in having their writing from this session collected into a booklet give their psalms to the designated collector or editor. *Do not pressure anyone to contribute.* Laments may be very personal and private, addressed only to God and not for public hearing.
- If a class member is willing to share what he or she has written, you might be able to use this as your closing prayer. The closing psalm could be read aloud by its author, or it could be passed around with each class member reading a different stanza. This choice should be made by the author of the closing psalm.
- If you prefer, end this session by reading Psalm 22:27-31 aloud to the class.

(G) Make a psalm into your own prayer.

- Those who prefer not to write a lament from scratch can try out the technique described in Chapter 6, "I," Option Two.
- Use the present form of Psalm 18:4-6 and 16-19 as the basis for a new prayer. First change the statements of distress in verses 4-6 into terms that make sense to you today. Next change any terms in verses 16-19 that seem to represent a worldview that is not your own into words that describe your own setting in life.
- Then change the statements in verses 16-19 that talk about God in the third person (he) into second person (you) statements. ("You reached down, you took me," and so on). In your final version begin with an address to God (such as found in Psalm 18:1), and end with an "Amen."

(H) Compare your own worldview with the psalmists' worldview.

- Use this option to continue the discussion begun in option "E."
- After you have reached some understanding about the conceptual content that the psalmists put into the word *Sheol*, ask people in your class to say how they think their own views about death differ from the views of the psalmists.
—Do you think having a different belief about death would have changed the tone of any of these psalms?
—Would having a different belief about death have changed the content of the petitions or requests that were addressed to God?
—Do you think people who believe in an afterlife show any less anguish about the prospect of leaving this life? Why, or why not? Should they, or should they not?
- If you have time, you may want to look at Psalm 29 as well as at Psalm 18 for images of the Lord as a God of the storm. After getting clear what phenomena are often said to accompany the appearance of the Lord on earth, discuss:
—What do you expect to see or hear when you are in God's presence?
—How would you expect to recognize a theophany (the coming of God to speak to humankind or to act on their behalf)?
—What do you think accounts for the differences between your expectations and the description found in Psalm 18?

(I) Examine how we use the Psalms in worship.

- This is an excellent opportunity to see how the psalms continue to empower our worship experiences. A closer look at the psalms in worship could prove very enlightening for your class.
- To find out how your congregation uses the psalms in worship you will need to bring hymnals and books of worship to class. If your church usually uses a lectionary cycle to choose biblical passages to be read in worship, bring a copy of the lectionary to class (your pastor, the church secretary, or your worship committee chairperson might have one, or there might be one in your church library). If possible, bring a collection of past bulletins that show the order of worship commonly used in your congregation.
- Divide class members into three groups.
—**Group One:** Ask this group to use the index in the back of your hymnals to see which psalms are used as the basis for hymns in your tradition. Ask group members to divide these up and look briefly at each psalm to see what kind of a psalm it is (a psalm of lament, a psalm of praise, a psalm of thanksgiving, and so on). Are any of the psalms studied in this session used in the hymnal?
—**Group Two:** Ask this group to examine the lectionary or the book of worship ordinarily used in your church. Are any of the psalms studied in this session listed or used? If so, which are used when, and where?
—**Group Three:** Ask the third group to look at old bulletins and see where (what place in the service) and how (in what form) psalms are used. Are they used as calls to worship, closings, as prayers of confession or praise, as responsive readings, or as a response to the (main) Scripture readings?
- Ask each group to report its findings back to the class in a summary statement.
- The study book points out that psalms such as 13, 22, and 88 are not commonly used in worship settings (except Psalm 22, which is often used on Good Friday). Is this also the case in your congregation? For a closer look at the psalms of lament that were studied today, discuss these questions:
—What implications might you draw from the fact that the psalms of lament or disorientation make up the largest category of psalms (over a third of the whole psalter is comprised of laments)?
—What implications might you draw from the fact that most of these laments are never used in Christian worship?
—Were you familiar with any of these psalms before you read them for this lesson? Do you wish you had been?
—Can you remember using any of these psalms in a worship setting? If so, describe the setting.
—Do you think the psalms of lament studied in this session should ever be used in a Christian worship setting? Why, or why not?
—Do you feel differently about Psalm 88 than about Psalm 13 or 22?
—How might Christians make the best use of Psalm 13? of Psalm 88?
—Is there any way we as church members can help increase the use of psalms or the breadth of selection of psalms used in our worship services?
- Close by reading Psalm 22:27-31.

Additional Bible Helps

Theophany
In the Book of Job, the Lord is said to speak to Job "out of the whirlwind" (Job 38:1, 40:6). When God appears to humankind in the Old Testament (in order to speak to people or to act in human history) the coming or the presence of God is often associated with fire, smoke, cloud (as in Exodus 13:21; 19:18; 24:17), or with wind, volcanic action, earthquake (as in Psalms 18 and 29; Judges 5:4-5, Habakkuk 3:3-15). But 1 Kings 19:9-12 makes it clear that

God is not actually seen or encountered in the wind, fire, smoke, earthquake, and so on. Rather, God's self-disclosure comes through the divine voice, which is heard in the midst of nature's turbulence.

The technical term used to describe the self-disclosure of God is *theophany* (thee-OF-un-nee), from the Greek words *theos* (God) and *phainein* (to appear). A theophany is a description of an occasion on which God appears or reveals God's self to humankind in order to speak or to act.

In the Old Testament, God is sometimes said to appear to people in human form, as in Genesis 18. But more often, God's self-disclosure is accompanied by turbulence in the atmosphere, as if nature itself is disturbed by the coming or the presence of God.

Old Testament theophanies are more often associated with thunderstorms than with any other natual phenomenon. This is true both in the prophetic and in the poetic texts. In the psalms, God is said to ride upon the storm clouds or on "the wings of the wind" (Psalms 18:10-11; 104:3), to speak with the voice of thunder (Psalms 18:13; 29:3), and to throw bolts of lightning like weapons against the enemies of Israel (Psalms 18:14; 29:7; 144:6).

Thunderstorms may have represented both the frightening and the comforting aspects of God's self-disclosure. Lightning, hail, and high winds were frightening and could bring death and destruction. But the rains contained in a thunderstorm could also bring life and comfort to a land that was constantly threatened by drought and famine. The psalmists can rejoice in the self-disclosure of God when the life-giving rains bring fertility to the land (Psalm 68:9) and when the destructive powers of the storm are turned against the enemies of Israel (Psalm 77:15-20).

Songs of Zion
Theophanies in the Old Testament are often said to take place on the top of mountains or "high places." In the historical narratives, Mount Sinai is often mentioned as the site of a theophany that had great significance in Israel's understanding of itself as a people claimed, chosen, and bound into a covenant relationship by the Lord. But in the period of the monarchy in Judah the importance of Mount Sinai was overshadowed by a mountain (or hill) known as Zion.

Zion was the name of the hill on which the ancient city that was later to be called Jerusalem was first built. David established his royal "house" or palace on Zion and Solomon built the first temple of the Lord on this promontory. Thus Zion was the location both of the center of government and of the center of religion in Judah.

Over the years, the term *Zion* gradually came to stand for the ruling presence of God on earth. God was said to "dwell" in Zion (Psalms 9:11; 76:2; and others). The Lord was "enthroned" as King in Zion (called the "hill of the LORD" in Psalm 24:3), and the Lord promoted righteousness and justice from Zion (Amos 1:2).

When the Northern Kingdom of Israel (with its capital in Samaria) fell to the Assyrians in the eighth century B.C., the Southern Kingdom of Judah (with its capital in Jerusalem) managed to escape destruction (apparently against all odds). The people of Judah attributed their survival as a nation-state to the presence of the Lord, who dwelt in the midst of them (on Zion). Thus they began to sing "Songs of Zion," which assumed that Jerusalem and its people were secure from all outside enemies, because the Temple of the Lord guaranteed the presence of the Lord in their midst (for example, Psalms 48; 87; 122). Jeremiah tried to warn his people that their confidence in the Temple building was misplaced (Jeremiah 7:3-4), but they refused to listen.

When Judah fell to the Babylonians, the Temple and the palace on Zion were destroyed and many Judeans were taken into Exile in Babylonia. In Psalm 137 the Babylonians taunt their captives by asking them to sing a "song of Zion," thus reminding them that their illusions about Zion had been shattered.

In the Book of Psalms, the term *Song of Zion* is usually applied to any psalm that glorifies either the "mountain of God" or the "city of God" (Jerusalem) as a place of security, a place in which God dwells, or from which God rules over the land (for instance, Psalms 46; 48; 76; 84; 87; 122).

After Judah ceased to be a nation in its own right, Mount Zion continued to be regarded as the place where God would someday appear in a storm-like setting to fight a final battle against all the forces of evil (Isaiah 66:6-16). After the destruction of the earthly Jerusalem, the faithful still looked forward to the day when God would rule over a world characterized by peace and justice (Isaiah 2:2-4). This is the Zion we envision when we sing, "We Are Marching to Zion."

8
Proverbs 1; 2; 8; 9

"Wisdom Cries Out in the Street"

LEARNING MENU

With this session we begin three units of study on the Book of Proverbs. Class members will have a chance to sample three of the distinctive styles of wisdom writing found in Proverbs, but the book itself contains many other items of interest. The following outline will help you see the "big picture."

The term *instruction* is borrowed from Egyptian wisdom texts that used this word for a similar type of wisdom writing (see "Additional Bible Helps." Chapter 10). The instructions all begin with an imperative that urges the pupil (called son or child) to pay attention. The speaker may be understood as a wisdom teacher or as Wisdom personified, giving advice to her "children."

Keeping in mind the ways your class members learn best, as well as their needs and interests, choose at least one learning segment from each of the three Dimensions.

OUTLINE OF PROVERBS

Prologue	1:1-7
Wisdom Instructions	1:8–9:18
First Instruction	1:8-19
Personified Wisdom Speaks	1:20-33
Ten More Instructions	2:1–7:27
Personified Wisdom Speaks	8:1-36
Wisdom and Folly Speak	9:1-18
375 Sentence Sayings	10:1–22:16
The "Sayings of the Wise"	22:17–24:34
The "Thirty Sayings"	22:17–24:22
Sayings Collected by Hezekiah's Men	25:1–29:27
The Words of Agur	30:1-33
The Words of Lemuel's Mother	31:1-31
Acrostic on the Strong Woman	31:10-31

Dimension 1: What Does the Bible Say?

(A) Hold an opening worship time.

- Gather class members together for a few moments of quiet time and a beginning Scripture reading. A passage that will go well with today's session is Proverbs 2:1-5.

(B) Answer Dimension 1 questions in the study book.

- If class members have not answered these questions ahead of time, provide a limited amount of time during which they can read the assigned Scripture passages and answer the questions.
  1. The first instruction (see earlier chart) illustrates the way wisdom teachers emphasize the automatic nature of retribution (without even mentioning God's role in the process). The wisdom teacher says violence is to be avoided because it "takes away the life of its possessors" (1:19).
  2. The most direct answer to this question is found in Proverbs 2:6 ("the LORD gives wisdom"). But it might also be argued that wisdom comes from the hard work involved in searching for it.
  3. In order to identify the "I" that speaks in Proverbs 8:22-31 you have to go back to Proverbs 8:12 where Wisdom identifies herself. Or go back to 8:1-3 where the wisdom teacher identifies her as the one who begins to speak in 8:4.
  4. Divide a section of the chalkboard or a large piece of paper into two columns and print "Wisdom" at the top of one and "Folly" at the top of the other column. As people share their answers to question 4, make a list of what Wisdom and Folly offer in Chapter 9. People's answers may differ considerably, depending on whether their answers are literal or analytical. For instance, an analytical answer might be "Wisdom offers people a challenge (to work hard to get insight) and Folly offers an easy way out." Be sure to note the similarity in the wording of 9:4 and 9:16.

(C) Roleplay the wisdom teacher and Wisdom personified.

- Ahead of time, get two sheets of paper of different colors (for instance, one piece of white and one of yellow).
- Cut each piece of paper into five strips. On one color of strips write the following:
—Why shouldn't I hang out with the gang on the street corner?
—Where does wisdom come from?
—How can I get wisdom and insight?
—What will having wisdom do for me?
—You are the wisdom teacher for this exercise.
- Write these on the strips of the second color:
—Why should I listen to you?
—What do you have to offer me?
—How do you know so much about the way the world works?
—How is what you offer me different from what Folly offers?
—You are Wisdom personified for this exercise.
- To begin the exercise, hand out strips randomly (or if you prefer, choose the people you think will do a good job with the roles of wisdom teacher and Wisdom personified).
- Have Wisdom personified and the wisdom teacher come to the front of the room, displaying their colors and identifying themselves to the whole class.
- Then ask the people who are holding the question strips to ask their questions of the appropriate person (according to the color of their paper).
- After the roleplay is complete, give the rest of the class a chance to discuss the answers given by Wisdom and the wisdom teacher. Were the answers given similar to the texts you read for today? How would others have answered the same questions?

Dimension 2: What Does the Bible Mean?

(D) Get familiar with the contents of Proverbs.

- Use the "Outline of Proverbs" (page 38, in this leader's guide) to make a chart (on posterboard or on a large piece of paper) large enough for the whole class to see. Post the chart where class members will be able to refer to it during the next two sessions as well.
- Ask people to open their Bibles and to look at Proverbs 1:1, 10:1, 25:1, 30:1, and 31:1. Discuss these questions with class members:
—What do these chapter headings seem to indicate about the material contained in the Book of Proverbs?
—Why do you think the same phrase "Proverbs of Solomon" is used three different times?
- Ask people to share their favorite proverb. If they do not know any biblical proverbs (which is quite likely), they can share a proverb they know from their own experience.
- If people have trouble coming up with proverbs, ask them to complete the following phrases:
—A stitch in time . . .
—You can lead a horse to water . . .

"WISDOM CRIES OUT IN THE STREET"

—Birds of a feather . . .
(You can probably think of others that are well known in your community. Share these briefly.)
- Then ask people to look again at some section of Proverbs 1–9.
- Next discuss these questions:
—Is the English title of Proverbs misleading?
—Do the materials in Chapters 1–9 sound anything like you expected Proverbs to sound?
—How would you explain to someone else why the title "Proverbs" has been given to this book? (If necessary, see the information in the study book about the semantic range of the Hebrew word *mashal*, Chapter 8, page 65.)
—If you were going to give a title to the material in Proverbs 1–9, what would you call it?

(E) Compare Old Testament images of creation.

- Write the following texts on the far left side of a chalkboard or a large piece of paper where everyone can see them.

Genesis 1:1-10	Psalm 136:5-9
Job 38:4-11	Proverbs 3:19-20
Psalm 33:6-7	Proverbs 8:25-30
Psalm 74:16-17	Isaiah 44:24
Psalm 104:5-6	Isaiah 48:13

- Assign each text to a person in your class to look up.
- Go around the room, reading the texts out loud in the order given. After each text is read, ask: "According to this text, what kind of action or actions did God perform in order to create the heavens, the earth, the seas, or the deeps?"
- To the right of the biblical citations on your chart, jot down the verbs used or implied in each passage.
- Discuss the similarities and the differences between these pictures of creation.
—Does the text in Proverbs 8 seem out of line (does it say something different) from the majority of these texts?
—What different kind of picture do you get of God's creative activity in Genesis 1 compared to most of the other texts?
—How do you account for the difference between these texts?
—Which of these images of creation was most familiar to you before hearing these texts read aloud?
—Why do you think the Genesis text has dominated our understanding of God's creative activity?

(F) Depersonalize the language in Proverbs 8.

- Bring a variety of biblical translations to class. Try to include a King James Version (KJV), a New International Version (NIV), a *New American Bible* (NAB), a *Jerusalem Bible* (JB), a *Good News Bible* (*The Bible in Today's English Version*, TEV), and a Revised Standard or New Revised Standard Version (RSV/NRSV).
- Distribute the different versions to various class members.
- Ask everyone to turn first to Proverbs 3:19-20.
- Read it aloud in your own version.
- Then ask class members to read along in their Bibles while you read aloud (from any version): Proverbs 8:1-2, 12, and 22-31.
- Then compare differences.
—Note that the KJV and NIV say in Proverbs 8:22: "The LORD *possessed* me in/at the *beginning* of his work," while the NAB says, "The LORD *begot* me, the *firstborn* of his ways," and RSV/NRSV say, "The LORD *created* me at the beginning of his work" (italics added).
- Now ask people to go back to the same verses you just read. Have someone read from each version available and *substitute* the words "The Wisdom of God" every place their texts have either *Wisdom* or a first-person pronoun (*I* or *me*) and to substitute the neuter pronoun (*it*) for every *she* or *her*. Thus instead of reading "Ages ago *I* was set up" (in 8:23), you will read "Ages ago *the wisdom of God* was set up." If you think this is too complicated for class members to do, you can prepare a substitution text ahead of time with your own version and read that to the class instead.
- Now discuss:
—What difference does it make to hear the text reread in this manner?
— How is your understanding of the text changed?

Dimension 3: What Does the Bible Mean to Us?

(G) Personalize the technique of personification.

- Bring to class visual examples of how we often use personification in our own culture (such as a Doonesbury cartoon strip about a large cigarette that tempts kids into smoking; a picture of "Uncle Sam"; a political cartoon showing a nation in the form of a person or an animal—such as Russia as a bear; a children's storybook or cartoon showing wind, sun, moon, and so on in animal form or with human features).
- Discuss:
—Why do we personifiy nonhuman things and ideas?
—What is the effect of having a personification speak directly to you?
—How do you think people who create personifications decide what characteristics should be given to the things they personify?

- Then divide class members into groups, separating women from men. And (if your class contains people from a variety of age groups and is large enough to do so) separate them into groups of younger women and older women, younger men and older men. Try to do this without letting people know that these are the categories you have in mind.
- Tell people to discuss and decide within their small group
—If Laziness were personified in our culture what form would it take?
—What would Laziness look like in human form?
—If you could sketch Laziness personified in a cartoon, what would Laziness be doing?
—What setting (physical surroundings) would you put the person Laziness in?
- Staying in the same groups, do the same excercise for Diligence personified. (If people are unsure of the meaning of *diligence*, define it for them as "hard-working, careful, doing work in a sustained and painstaking manner.")
- Ask each group to report back to the whole class, describing their "picture" in detail.
- Then ask everyone to evaluate all the groups' work:
—What gender (male or female) did the men's group (or groups) assume for Laziness? for Diligence?
—What gender did the women's group (or groups) assume for their personifications?
—Were the personifications of Laziness conceived to be from the same or from different age groups or from the same or from different racial/ethnic/class backgrounds as their creators?
—How about the personifications of Diligence?
—Would these personifications be easily understood in other cultures, by people whose resources, customs, or lifestyles were very different?
- Your group may prove to be unusual, but chances are good that people will assign Laziness to their opposite gender and Diligence to their own gender. Positive values are likely to be conceived as being "like me," and negative values are more likely to be personified as people "not like me."
- Discuss with your class:
—What new ideas have occurred to you after doing this exercise?
—Do you think the personifications in Proverbs reflect the social, political, and cultural assumptions of the people who created them?
—If so, what does this imply for our understanding of the material?
—Do you think the wisdom teacher who speaks in Proverbs 8 might have been a woman?
- Explain: In Hebrew, as in English, first person pronouns (*I, me, we*) are the same for men and women. A woman could be the *I* who speaks anywhere in Proverbs 1–9, except in Chapter 4, because of the comment in 4:3. However, the situation is somewhat complicated because the Hebrew language assigns gender to all nouns (all nouns are either masculine or feminine, there is no neuter). Since the words for Wisdom and Folly are both feminine nouns, it may have been more difficult for anyone (even men) to conceive of Wisdom personified as anything other than a woman. Nevertheless, we can assume that the specific characteristics that Wisdom takes on are a product of the cultural and social assumptions of those who "painted her picture" in Proverbs.
—Do you think the personification of Wisdom as a woman makes "her" more attractive in our own culture to women or to men?
- End with a prayer that you address to the Wisdom of God (for example, beginning "O Wisdom of God, be with us today . . .").

(H) Consider the development of the Nicene Creed.

- You will need copies of the Nicene Creed for this activity. You will find the Nicene Creed in the Affirmations of Faith section of *The United Methodist Hymnal*, 880.
- Find a copy of the *New American Bible* (or another translation that uses *begot* in Proverbs 8:22), and bring it to class along with several other translations.
- Write the terms *Arianism* and *Nicea* on the board or on a large piece of paper. Be prepared to present a summary of the essential points of the Arian controversy for your class from the information in the box below.

> The Arians were a prominent group in early Christianity (fourth century A.D.) who stood against the doctrine of the Trinity. Because of a concern for the one-ness of God, the Arians asserted that God's son was subordinate, not equal to God. They argued that the Son was created, one of God's works, not of the same substance as God. Since New Testament passages sometimes equated Christ with Wisdom, the Arians used Proverbs 8:22 as a proof-text for their position. The church council held at Nicea in 325 A.D. declared Arianism a heresy and produced the Nicean (Nicene) Creed, which declares that Christ was "begotten, not made" and that the Son was "one in essence" ("of one Being") with the Father.

- Read Proverbs 8:22-31 aloud. Ask class members to compare translations of 8:22, 30-31. Then ask this question:
—What different impressions do you get of Wisdom's status and role in creation from the different versions?
- Next hand out copies of the Nicene Creed, and close this session by reading the creed in unison.

Additional Bible Helps

Wisdom in the Apocrypha

In Bibles published by and for Protestant Christians you will sometimes find a separate section of materials called "the Apocrypha" placed in between the Old and the New Testament. The word *Apocrypha* (uh-POK-ruh-fuh) means "things hidden away." In Bibles published by and for Roman Catholic Christians, these same materials can be found distributed among the other books of the Old Testament, according to literary types. Catholics call these books "Deuterocanonical" (dyoo-tuh-roh-kuh-NON-i-kuhl), implying that they belong to a second (but still authoritative) layer in the development of the canon.

The Septuagint (SEP-too-uh-jint, the Greek Bible used by the early Christian church) contained a number of books that were later excluded from the Hebrew canon. In the first and second centuries after Christ, Jewish religious authorities insisted that only those ancient books that were written originally in Hebrew, before or during the time of Ezra, could be regarded as authoritative Scripture. But early Christians accepted a number of additional books into their canon of the Old Testament. At the time of the Reformation, Protestants adopted the shorter Hebrew canon, while Roman Catholics continued to affirm the longer version.

If you look at a Catholic edition of the Bible (such as *The New American Bible* or *The Jerusalem Bible*) you will find that two other books of ancient wisdom literature are listed right after The Song of Solomon in these editions. The first is called either "The Book of Wisdom" or "The Wisdom of Solomon," and the second is called either "The Book of Sirach" or "Ecclesiasticus." These two books (plus a section of a third book, called Baruch, found immediately after Lamentations) have many features in common with Job, Proverbs, and Ecclesiastes. Even if they are considered "apocryphal" (and thus not "authoritative" for religious purposes) they should be included in any thorough study of the Wisdom Literature of Israel.

Jesus ben Sirach (Jesus, son of Sirach) was a wisdom teacher who taught in Jerusalem around 180 B.C. His book seems to have been modeled for the most part after Proverbs and has the same variety of instructional and proverbial material in it. Like Proverbs, Sirach praises the fear of the Lord as the source and foundation of wisdom (Sirach 1:11-30). Unlike the authors of Proverbs, Sirach makes a number of recognizable allusions to people and events in the history of Israel, particularly in his lengthy hymn entitled "Praise of Our Ancestors" in Chapters 44–50.

The Wisdom of Solomon pretends to be an autobiography of the idealized Solomon, who was said to be continually engaged in a search for wisdom. In fact, however, it was written sometime in the century before the beginning of the Christian era. The Wisdom of Solomon is more like Ecclesiastes than Proverbs. Its author was familiar with Hellenistic (Greek) culture and Greek philosophical ideas, such as the Greek distinction between body and soul (9:14-15). This book emphasizes the mercy of God, explaining any perceived delay in the punishment of the wicked as an attempt on God's part to give people time to repent (11:23–12:11). Like Sirach, the Wisdom of Solomon refers to people and events in Israel's history. But according to the Wisdom of Solomon, Wisdom personified (*Sophia* in the Greek text) played an essential part in the story of Israel's salvation.

The Personification of Wisdom

The figure of Personified Wisdom appears in Sirach, in the Wisdom of Solomon, and in Baruch 3:9–4:4, as well as in Proverbs 1:20-33, 8:1-31, 9:1-6.

In Proverbs, Wisdom seems to be a personification of one of the Lord's attributes.

In Sirach, Wisdom speaks for and about herself much as she did in Proverbs 8. She says she "came forth from the mouth of the Most High" (Sirach 24:3) and was commissioned by God to make her home in Israel and to "take root" among God's chosen people (Sirach 24:8-9, see also Baruch 3:36).

But in the Wisdom of Solomon the personified Wisdom is an active guiding force who is so closely identified with God that it is difficult sometimes to distinguish between them. She seems to be identical with (or interchangeable with) God's Holy Spirit. Wisdom "was present when thou [God] didst make the world" (Wisdom 9:9). She is "a breath of the power of God, / and a pure emanation of the glory of the Almighty" (7:25) as well as "a spotless mirror of the working of God" (7:26). She "can do all things, . . . she renews all things" (7:27). In Israel's history, it was Wisdom who protected Adam (10:1); abandoned Cain (10:3); saved Noah (10:4), Abraham (10:5), Lot (10:6), Jacob (10:10-12), and Joseph (10:13-14). Wisdom inspired Moses (10:16) and made the Exodus from Egypt a reality (10:17-21).

In Greek-speaking Jewish communities and in the early church, the terms *Sophia* (meaning Wisdom) and *Logos* (meaning Word) were used interchangeably as symbols of the workings of God in the world. Thus Jewish wisdom imagery helped shape John's concept of Christ as the Logos/Word of God. Many of the things that were said about wisdom in these apocryphal books were later said about Jesus Christ, who was identified with both the Wisdom and the Word of God in the Gospel of John and in the letters of Paul.

"Wisdom Is a Fountain of Life"

LEARNING MENU

Keeping in mind the ways your class members learn best, as well as their needs and interests, choose at least one learning segment from each of the three Dimensions.

Dimension 1: What Does the Bible Say?

(A) Hold an opening worship.

- Gather class members together by singing. A suggested song is "Come, Thou Fount of Every Blessing," *The United Methodist Hymnal*, 400.

(B) Answer Dimension 1 questions in the study book.

1. Ask people to identify (by verse number) which sayings they found most interesting in Chapter 10. If several were interested in the same verse, begin by reading that verse in one or two translations. Then ask the people who chose this verse to share their attempts to paraphrase this saying (to restate the point in their own words).

    Continue sharing favorite verses and paraphrases for a few minutes until everyone who wants to contribute has had a chance to do so.

2. Again, have people identify their choices by verse number and if several people agree on one verse, begin by reading that one aloud. Be sure to ask people *why* they particularly agreed or disagreed with the verse.

3. Most of what Chapter 16 has to say about the Lord is found in the first eleven verses and in the last verse (16:33). It may be best to group some verses together for discussion purposes. It seems that 16:1, 3-4, 9, and 33 are on the subject of God's complete control over what happens in the world. The "lot" mentioned in 16:3 was used to "inquire of the LORD," to see who was guilty (Jonah 1:7), or how to divide up the land among the tribes (Joshua 14:2), and so on. Verse 2 refers to God's ability to judge one's true motives for doing something, and verses 8 and 11 have to do with social justice or honest and dishonest business practices.

CASTING LOTS

The Israelites often used lots as a method of determining the will of God. The priest carried two inscribed stones, called Urim and Thummim (lights and perfections), that were thrown in doubtful cases so the entire nation would know God's will. Casting lots was commonly preceded by prayer (from *Joshua, Judges, Ruth*, volume 3 of JOURNEY THROUGH THE BIBLE, page 33).

---

4. Most people will recognize 25:21-22, and some will recognize 25:24. Ask: Why do you know the sayings you found familiar?

(C) Compare translations and paraphrases.

- For this activity you will need three different colors of paper. Copy onto the paper a few verses that you found interesting in this chapter, using *The Living Bible* (which is a paraphrase) and/or the *Good News Bible* (which is a translation that tries to catch the essential sense of proverbial sayings). Use one color of paper for verses from Chapter 10, another for verses from Chapters 13–14, and a third color for verses from Chapter 16. Be sure to note down for yourself which color represents which chapter. Instead of using colored paper, you could write the chapter number next to each verse you copy, but do not include the verse numbers. Cut the paper into pieces or strips so that each strip contains only one unnumbered verse (like fortunes in fortune cookies).
- Give each participant one or more verses, depending on the size of the class. (You do not want this exercise to take up the whole session.)
- Take turns having one person read aloud from his or her piece of paper while the rest of the class looks in their own Bibles and tries to identify which verse in their translation corresponds to the verse being read. (Do not let anyone else use either the *Good News Bible* or *The Living Bible*.)
- A less complicated (and perhaps less entertaining) way of accomplishing the same purpose is for you to read a verse or two (one at a time) from each chapter of today's assigned biblical texts, using either *The Living Bible* or the *Good News Bible* as your text, while class members try to guess which verse in their own translations corresponds to the one you are reading.

(D) Create a proverbial picture.

- Ahead of time collect a variety of pictures from magazines and catalogues, coupons or advertisements on glossy paper. Bring these pictures to class, along with scissors, glue, construction paper or posterboard, and colored markers. Try to find pictures of people laughing, crying, working, sleeping; weights (scales), lights, lamps, fires, fountains; trees; honey; vinegar; a dog, a door, a lion.

- As an example to show class members you might prepare a picture with "PLEASANT WORDS" at the top and a pot of honey beneath, with Proverbs 16:24 written on the back of the paper.
- Divide class members into pairs or small groups.
- Give groups ten to fifteen minutes to choose and picture one of the proverbs read for today, using at most one or two words and the rest graphic images (either drawn by hand or cut from printed materials).
- On the back of each paper (the side away from the illustration) ask each group to write the chapter and verse number of its selection.
- Ask each group to share its results, asking others to guess what proverb is pictured.

Dimension 2: What Does the Bible Mean?

(E) Consider the implications of figurative language.

Part One:
- In keeping with the title of this chapter ("Wisdom Is a Fountain of Life"), begin by listing Proverbs 13:14, 14:27, and 16:22 on the chalkboard or a large piece of paper.
- Look these verses up and read them out loud.
- Next to each verse number, note what different things are said to be "a fountain of life."
—What do you think "fountain of life" means or implies in these sayings? (Longer life or better quality of life or what?)
—Do you take the term *life* literally or figuratively in these sayings?
—What do you conclude from the fact that the teaching of the wise, the fear of the Lord, and wisdom are *all* said to be "a fountain of life?"
- Next look up and read Proverbs 10:16-17, 27. Then discuss what "life" seems to mean in each of these sayings.
- Look up and read Proverbs 16:24, 25:16, and 25:27.
—What is "honey" equated with in 25:27? in 16:24?
—If you understand the word *honey* figuratively (as a way of referring to "honor upon honor" or perhaps "pleasant words" [meaning flattery?]) and then reread 25:16, what does the saying in 25:16 now seem to be about?

Part Two:

- For this part of the actitivy, you will need to do some preparations before the session. Either use some of the "proverbial pictures" from option "D" or make some posters yourself ahead of time. Cut out pictures from magazines and newspapers for all the figurative terms listed below (a fountain, a pot of honey or a honeycomb, burning coals or charcoal, a trap or a pit, and so on), and put each picture on a piece of construction paper along with the chapter and verse numbers of the saying it represents.
- Post the pictures around the classroom.

- Discuss the literal and figurative meanings of the following:
  — "coals of fire" in 25:22
  — "light" and "lamp" in 13:9 (See Job 18:5 and 21:17.)
  — "rod" in 13:24
  — "pit" and "stone" in 26:27
- As class members decide on various meanings for the terms used in the sayings, use a marker pen to add these meanings to the appropriate pictures.

(F) Consider the collector's differing opinions.

- Look at these pairs of verses: 13:22 and 13:23; 14:20 and 14:21; 26:4 and 26:5; 10:15 and 10:16. Each pair represents a disagreement between two sayings (or two speakers).
- Ask class members to look at each pair in turn and to discuss the differences.
— The last pair listed above (10:15 and 10:16) may be the most difficult to deal with. If people find it hard to see the area in which these two verses disagree, ask them to consider "What leads to life?" (Verse 16 says being righteous does, but verse 15 implies that anyone with wealth, whether they are righteous or not, can find a protective "fortress" in that wealth.) Similarly, if you ask "what leads to ruin?" you can answer "poverty" (10:15) or "the gain of the wicked" (10:16).
- Point out also what the study book says about the variety of opinions represented in the "Collective Sayings of the Wise" (page 73).

(G) Examine the meaning of oblique sayings.

Many popular proverbs in our culture are oblique or indirect, not stating directly what they mean. "Penny wise, pound foolish" is a good example of an oblique saying that can be taken to refer to many different kinds of human behavior.
- Ask class members to consider the ways in which the following biblical proverbs communicate meaning.
- Begin by reading out loud a series of humorous sayings about laziness (Proverbs 26:13-15).
— What is the point being made in 26:13?
— Why would a lazy person say, "There is a lion in the streets"?
— What terms are parallel (poetically synonymous with each other) in 26:14?
— What is it about the door on its hinges that is like a lazy person in bed? (A number of possibilities may be noted.)
— Is 26:15 simply descriptive or is there a hidden warning here about the fate of the lazy person?

- Read 26:17 and discuss what similarities there are between the things that are compared in its two lines.
- Do the same for 26:22
- Read 27:27. Do you think the point in this verse is clear or oblique? Would you say that this proverb is
  (a) never true?
  (b) always true?
  (c) sometimes true?
- Try to paraphrase the point in 26:27 (restate its essential meaning in other words). This saying was a very popular one in ancient Near Eastern cultures. We have examples of its usage in some of the Egyptian Instructions and in the Apocryphal Wisdom of Sirach (27:26) as well as in Ecclesiastes 10:8a and Psalm 7:15.

Dimension 3:
What Does the Bible Mean to Us?

(H) Sift through "timely" and timeless sayings.

- Reread or review the section in the study book that deals with the situation-specific nature of proverbs ("Is the Advice Timely or Timeless?" page 75).
- Divide your chalkboard or a large piece of paper into two columns, labeled "Timely" and "Timeless."
- Briefly discuss the meaning of these terms. (*Timely* refers to sayings that apply only to some situations or are true only under certain circumstances; *timeless* refers to statements that seem to be universally true, true in all conceivable circumstances, applicable in all situations everywhere.)
- Divide into six groups. Assign each group one of the chapters studied for today (10; 13; 14; 16; 25; 26).
- Ask participants to suggest one or two sayings from the chapter assigned to them that seem to them to be "timely" (applicable only to some situations) and one or two sayings that seem to them to be "timeless" (universally true).
- Or ask the whole class to suggest sayings that seem to them to fit into one category or another. If people are slow to respond, prime the pump by asking them what they think Job would have said about Proverbs 13:9 ("the lamp of the wicked goes out"). If they have forgotten what Job said, have them turn to Job 21:17, 29-30.
- Then ask whether they think this saying in Proverbs 13:9 is timely or timeless. How about 16:2, 16:7, 16:18, or 16:31? Be open to the possibility of disagreement on these issues.
- Here are some questions to add to the discussion:
— What is needed to make a saying "timeless"?
— Does the fact that Paul quoted Proverbs 25:21-22a (Romans 12:20) give this saying some special status?

(I) Distinguish between descriptive and prescriptive proverbs.

- Divide your chalkboard or a large piece of paper into two columns, labeled "Descriptive" and "Prescriptive."
- Briefly discuss the meaning of these terms as they are used in the study book ("Descriptive Statements on Life," page 74). *Descriptive* statements describe or comment on something that is or was. *Prescriptive* statements say that something should be or ought to be the case.
- Read through Proverbs 25:11-28, one verse at a time.
- At the end of each verse ask class members to decide if they think this saying is descriptive or prescriptive.
- Write the verse numbers in the appropriate columns.
- Look at the sayings you have listed as prescriptive. (Verses 16-17, 21 are the only clearly prescriptive sayings in this section.)
—What kinds of reasons are given to explain why you should do what the proverb says you should do?
—Do you think the reason given in 25:22 is an admirable reason?
- Take a few of the descriptive sayings in this section, and ask people to draw prescriptive conclusions based on the proverbial descriptions.
—Do this by adding "therefore . . ." to the end of the saying. For example, you might add the following on to the end of 25:20a, "Therefore, if you don't want to be considered as irritating as vinegar in a wound, don't sing songs to someone who has a heavy heart."
- Do the same for 16:2, 16:8, 16:11, and 16:18.
—What process of reasoning do you have to go through in order to make a descriptive proverb into a prescriptive saying?
—First you have to decide that the proverb's description seems to ring true in your experience.
—Do you agree, for instance, that "Whoever digs a pit will fall into it" (26:27)? If so, then you might decide that you do not want to fall into a pit and thus will avoid digging one in order to entrap someone else.
—However, if you are like Job and can think of many cases in which this descriptive statement did not hold true in your experience, then you will probably not allow the saying to have prescriptive force in your life.
—Do the prescriptive sayings in the Book of Proverbs have any moral force for you? Does anything urge you or compel you to comply with any of the Proverbs you have read today? Why, or why not?

(J) Study two New Testament references to Proverbs.

- Recruit three readers, one for each of these Scripture passages: Romans 12:14-20; Matthew 5:43-46; and Proverbs 25:21-22a.
- Ask each reader to read aloud her or his passage of Scripture.
- Then discuss these questions:
—What is Paul trying to convince people to do?
—What is Jesus trying to convince people to do?
—What does Paul say or imply about God's nature in this passage? Does he assume God will punish the unrighteous?
—How does Paul's use of Proverbs 25:21-22a fit into his argument?
—Does Proverbs 25:21-22 say or imply that God will take vengeance on the enemies?
—What does Jesus say about God's nature in this passage? What does Jesus say God does to the unrighteous?

(K) Decide what leads to life.

- Look at the chart in the study book ("What Leads to Life?" page 77) that "samples" the shorter sayings by grouping them according to subject matter.
- Depending on the size of your class, you can either assign different topics from the chart to different people, divide into groups and assign one topic to each group, or allow people to choose their own topics. (Not all topics need to be covered.)
- Set a time limit so that you will have ten to fifteen minutes for discussion and closing time after people have finished their work.
- Assure people that it is okay if they only have time to sample some of the passages listed. It is desirable, but not necessary, to look up all the references on their subject in order to get an idea of the proverbialists' opinions.
- Ask people to note anything that stands out as particularly interesting or unexpected in the verses they read.
- Come back into a whole group, and ask each person or a spokeperson for each group to summarize in general terms what the wise in Israel thought about the topic they have investigated and any unusual or surprising items they noted along the way.
- When all groups or individuals have reported, discuss some of the following:
—Do the sentence sayings in the Book of Proverbs have any moral force for you?
—Does anything urge you or compel you to comply with any of the Proverbs you have read today?
—Why, or why not?
—What kind of authority do the biblical Proverbs have for us today?
—How do you go about deciding what biblical proverbs are "wise" or useful for you today?

(L) Close with a worship time.

- A suggestion for closing worship is to offer sentence prayers of petition based on the Proverbs. An example is "Help us to be steadfast in righteousness" (Proverbs 11:19).

Additional Bible Helps

Translation Problems in Proverbs

All translations are to some extent interpretations. It is impossible to move from the words of an ancient Near Eastern language like Hebrew into a modern, western language like English without adding to, subtracting from, or changing in some way the original sense of many statements. It is especially difficult for translators to capture the original flavor of poetic and proverbial texts.

Both proverbs and poetry get an essential part of their meaning from the sounds and the patterns of the words they use. The *thought* expressed in a saying such as "Birds of a feather flock together" is not particularly profound. We remember the proverb and repeat it as much for its pleasing sound combination as for the thought it contains.

But the combination of sound and meaning is impossible to capture in translation from one language into another. Furthermore, proverbs and poetry often use ambiguous words or phrases. The translator has to consider what meaning is communicated to the listener by obscure and ambiguous phrases like "of a feather" before an attempt can be made to translate the thought of this saying into another language. Translators cannot go to the original speaker of a biblical proverb and ask, "What did you mean when you said this?"

Languages have different degrees of precision in different areas of thought. People who live in moderate or warm climates may have only one word for "snow," but people who live around the polar cap have a number of words to designate different types of snow. Hebrew has at least three words that are translated into the single English word *fool*. Modern translators are not able to distinguish between the finer nuances of meaning that distinguished one fool from another in Hebrew proverbs. We can only guess at the distinctions based on what the proverbs say about them. Thus we are told that fine speech is wasted on a *nabal*/fool and that the parents of such a fool have "no joy" (17:21). The *kesil*/fool considers wrongdoing laughable (10:23), hates to turn away from evil (13:19), indulges in self-deception (14:8), and does not learn from punishment (17:10). The *ewil*/fool does not "heed the commandments" (10:8), will not listen to advice (12:15), and also "despises" parental authority (15:5).

Translations of the biblical text are also affected by the social and personal biases of the translators themselves. Translators are fallible human beings just like anyone else. One obvious example of this can be found in Proverbs 2:16, 5:3, 5:20, and 7:5. In the RSV, NRSV, and NIV these passages all seem to warn the young wisdom student to avoid women who are sexually promiscuous. While this may be wise advice in general, the sense of the original warning has been radically changed in these translations.

The terms *loose woman*, *adulteress*, *adventuress*, and *wayward wife* are used in these versions to translate two Hebrew words, which both have the essential meaning of "foreignness" or "strangeness." When these Hebrew words occur elsewhere in the Old Testament they are always understood as references to "foreigners," "aliens," or "strangers." Psalm 81:9 uses both these words properly: "There shall be no *strange* god among you; / you shall not bow down to a *foreign* god" (italics added). Nehemiah 10:30 and Ezra 10:2-44 repeatedly use the same words to refer to the foreign women who had become the wives of Israelite men after the destruction of Jerusalem by the Babylonians.

The original words used in the Hebrew text refer to women who are either not of Israelite origins or not worshipers of God. It is true that Old Testament texts sometimes use metaphors such as *harlotry* and *adultery* to refer to Israel's relationships with the gods of other nations. The covenant relationship between Israel and God can be compared to a marriage. If Israel is "married" to God, then any relationship with another god (idolatry) can be understood as unfaithfulness or adultery. Unfaithfulness to the covenant can be called adultery. However, foreignness itself is not adulterous. The translators have mistakenly assumed that non-Israelite women are sexually promiscuous, while non-Israelite men are not. This can be seen most easily in Proverbs, Chapter 5. In 5:3 the feminine singular word *zarah* is translated "loose" woman in the NRSV, while in 5:10 the very same word, only in the masculine plural, is translated "strangers." In 5:20 the feminine singular word *nokriyyah* is translated "adulteress," while in 5:10 the masculine form of the same word is translated "alien."

The original Hebrew text urges the wisdom student to choose fidelity, to remain faithful to Wisdom (who is his real "wife"). If the student who is married to the way of wisdom follows any other way of life, *he* will be an adulterer. Thus the translators have changed the whole sense of the wisdom teacher's advice by labeling only *her* the sinner.

10 "The Eyes of the Lord Keep Watch Over Knowledge"

Proverbs 22–23; 30–31

LEARNING MENU

Keeping in mind the ways your class members learn best, as well as their needs and interests, choose at least one learning segment from each of the three Dimensions.

Dimension 1: What Does the Bible Say?

(A) Open with a time of worship.

- Begin today's session by having different people (one per verse) read from Proverbs 22. Ask each reader to read one verse, with a time of silence between each reading. Some suggested verses to include are 22:1, 2, 4, 6, 8, and 9.

(B) Answer Dimension 1 questions in the study book.

- Discussion of the Dimension 1 questions might lead in these directions:
  1. Now that students have read and discussed quite a few chapters of Proverbs, many of the sayings will begin to sound familiar. Several of the sayings in Chapter 22 (particularly verses 6-8) are well known to modern audiences. People also may notice that 22:13 is a duplicate of 26:13 (the lion in the streets), and 22:3 will be repeated in 27:12. The use of the "rod" for discipline is mentioned again in 22:15 and 23:13-14, as it was in 13:24. The sayings in 22:28 and 23:10 are similar to each other and to 15:25. The sayings in 22:14 and 23:27 are similar to 2:16-17 and 5:3-5.
  2. As you are answering this question, you may want to look closely at the images used in this description of the alcoholic in 23:29-35. (For instance, does 23:33 refer to delirium tremens?)
  3. Answers include "things that never say, 'Enough' " (30:15-16), "things that are too wonderful for me" (30:18-19, "things that cause the earth to tremble" (30:21-23), "things that are small but wise" (30:24-28), and "things that are stately in their stride" (30:29-31). Four things are also listed without a heading that says what they have in common in 30:11-14.
  4. The husband specifically praises his incredible wife in 31:29 ("Many women have done excellently, but you surpass them all"). The speaker tells him he should "give her a share in the fruit of her hands, / and let her works praise her in the city gates" (31:31).

(C) Share the best and the worst of the sayings.

- Divide your class into pairs or into groups of three people each.
- Ask people to share with each other which of the sayings

48

JOURNEY THROUGH THE BIBLE

in Chapters 22–23 and 30–31 they liked the best and which they liked the least (or were somewhat offended by).
- Ask them also to share what it was about the saying that caused them to feel the way they do about it.
- Come back into the larger group and list on chalkboard or on a large piece of paper what people liked the best.
- Look to see if more than one person liked one particular saying. If so, ask why this one appealed to people.
- Ask other class members what they thought about it and why.
- List what people liked the least in today's reading. Again, if several people chose the same thing, ask what it was they disliked and then ask other people what they thought about this saying.

(D) Compare Bible translations and paraphrases.

- For this activity you will need four sheets of paper, each a different color. Copy on the paper a few verses you found interesting in this chapter's Scripture, using the versions of these verses in *The Living Bible* (which is a paraphrase) and/or the *Good News Bible* (which is a translation that tries to catch the essential sense of proverbial sayings).
- Use one color of paper for verses from Proverbs 22, another color of paper for verses from Chapter 23, a third color of paper for verses from Chapter 30 and a fourth color of paper for verses from Chapter 31. Be sure to note which color represents which chapter. Instead of using colored paper, you may write the chapter number next to each verse you copy, but do not include the verse numbers.
- Cut the paper into pieces or strips so that each strip contains only one unnumbered verse (like fortunes in fortune cookies).
- Give each participant one or more verses, depending on the size of the class. (You do not want this exercise to take up the whole session.)
- Take turns having one person read his or her verse aloud while the rest of the class look in their own Bibles and try to identify which verse in their translation corresponds to the verse being read. (Do not let anyone use either a *Good News Bible* or *The Living Bible* for their reference text.)
- A less complicated (and perhaps less entertaining) way of accomplishing the same purpose is for you to read a verse or two (one at a time) from each chapter of today's assigned biblical texts, using either *The Living Bible* or a *Good News Bible* as your text, while class members try to guess which verse in their own translations corresponds to the one you are reading.

Dimension 2:
What Does the Bible Mean?

(E) Explore proverbial attitudes toward alcoholic drinks.

In the Old Testament, wine is often understood to be a common beverage, something that might legitimately be used by people celebrating the Lord's blessings on them (Deuteronomy 14:26 and Proverbs 9:2, 5). A certain amount of wine was supposed to be poured out as "a drink offering" (given to God) on a regular basis (Exodus 29:40; Leviticus 23:13).

However, Old Testament witnesses were quite aware of the negative effects of intoxication. The people set apart or dedicated to God as Nazirites (NAZ-uh-ritez) were forbidden to drink intoxicating beverages (Numbers 6:2-3). The word translated "to be or become drunk" is sometimes used as a figure of speech for being helpless and disgraced (Psalms 60:3; 107:27; Jeremiah 48:26).
- Divide class members into four groups, and assign each group one of the following sets of verses:
—**Group One:** Proverbs 20:1; 21:17; 26:10
—**Group Two:** Proverbs 23:20-21
—**Group Three:** Proverbs 23:29-35
—**Group Four:** Proverbs 31:4-7
- Ask each group to decide the answers to the following questions:
—Do these verses say anything positive about alcoholic beverages? If so, what?
—Do these verses condemn all use of alcoholic beverages? If so, then how do these verses fit alongside such other verses as Proverbs 9:2, 5?
—What do these verses say is the problem with the excess use of intoxicating beverages?
- After hearing these reports, ask the whole group to discuss:
—How would you summarize the attitude taken by the contributors to Proverbs concerning "strong drink"?

(F) Decide if some proverbial sayings are sacred or secular.

The purpose of this activity is to have class members understand in a new way the ongoing development of wise and proverbial sayings. Society continues to highlight wise sentences and sayings from everyday language and speech. We need to be alert and know that not all wise-sounding sayings are sacred (from the Bible).
- *Advance preparation*: Select from the following list which proverbial sayings you want your class to explore. Then copy each saying onto a piece of paper or an index card. On the back of the paper or card write the author or the Proverbs reference. You will need a sheet of paper to

place beside each card. Draw two columns on each sheet of paper. Label one column "Sacred" (in the Bible) and the other column "Secular." You will need pencils or pens for the voting.
- Post the sayings, along with an accompanying sheet of paper, around your classroom. Mix up the sayings so the secular sayings and sacred sayings are not all together.
- Ask class members to walk around the room, read the sayings, and "vote" whether the proverbial saying is sacred or secular by placing a mark in the appropiate column.
- Another way to do this would be to write each saying at the top of a sheet of paper, make two columns below the saying, and pass the sheets around to class members.
- After the voting, reveal the results.
—Which quotations surprised class members?
—Do we ever take the secular wise sayings and claim them to be biblical? (The Ben Franklin quotation is a good example of this.)
— Discuss with class members the role proverbial sayings play in our society.
- Here are some sayings to choose from:
—Two heads are better than one. (John Heywood, *Proverbs*; 1546)
—When Fortune means to men most good, / She looks upon them with a threatening eye. (William Shakespeare, *King John*, Act III, Scene iv)
—God helps them that help themselves. (Benjamin Franklin, *Poor Richard's Almanac*; 1736)
—God's in his heaven; all's right with the world. (Robert Browning, "Pippa Passes"; 1841)
—You give little when you give of your possessions. It is when you give of yourself that you truly give. (Kahlil Gibran, "On Giving," *The Prophet;* 1924)
—God gives us grace to accept with serenity the things that cannot be changed, courage to change the things which should be changed, and the wisdom to distinguish the one from the other. (Reinhold Niebuhr, *The Serenity Prayer;* 1943)
—A hungry [person] is not a free [person]. (Adlai Ewing Stevenson, Speech at Kasson, Minnesota; September 6, 1952)
—The road to hell is paved with good intentions. (H. G. Bohn, *Hand-Book of Proverbs;* 1855)
—When one is a stranger to oneself then one is estranged from others too. (Anne Morrow Lindbergh, *Gift from the Sea;* 1955)
—Injustice anywhere is a threat to justice everywhere. (Martin Luther King, Jr., *Letter from the Birmingham Jail;* 1963)
—Apply your mind to instruction / and your ear to the words of knowledge. (Proverbs 23:12)
—All the days of the poor are hard, / but a cheerful heart has a continual feast. (Proverbs 15:15)
- Add some selections of your own from the Book of Proverbs to add to the activity. (See chart on page 72 for help.)

(G) Create your own paraphrase.

Proverbs 31:10-31
- The poem about the strong woman or the ideal wife in Proverbs 31:10-31 has twenty-two verses (the same as the number of letters in the Hebrew alphabet). Divide these verses evenly among the members of your class. If you have more than twenty-two participants, ask some people to work in pairs or small groups.
- Ask each group to use its own words to express the meaning of the assigned verse in one short sentence.
- If you wish you can suggest that they make a *modern* paraphrase. (What would this activity be called in the life of a modern person?)
- Read the whole poem out loud, verse by verse, in its newly paraphrased version.

Assorted Sayings
- Or you may choose to ask class members to choose which verses or passages they would like to "update" or put into modern terms. This could be done in pairs, trios, or in small groups as well as by individuals.
- After sharing each paraphrase with the whole group, ask people to say whether they had understood the original text in a significantly different way than the paraphraser did.

Dimension 3:
What Does the Bible Mean to Us?

(H) Find out how women are portrayed in Proverbs.

Consider the various ways women are portrayed in Proverbs.
- Reread and prepare to present to class members the information about the terms *loose woman* and *adulteress* that is found in the "Additional Bible Helps" of Chapter 9 (page 47).
- Ask class members what their overall impressions are concerning the way women have been portrayed in Proverbs. See what people remember from their reading.

Part One
- Divide class members into four groups to review the following passages:
  Group One: Wisdom personified: Proverbs 1:20-33; 8:1-36
  Group Two: Folly personified: Proverbs 9:13-18
  Group Three: The strong woman/wife: Proverbs 31:10-31; 12:4
  Group Four: Sentence sayings about wives: 18:22; 19:13; 19:14; 21:9, 19; 25:24; 27:15
- Ask a spokesperson from each group to summarize the way women are portrayed in the passage or passages the group has just reviewed.

Part Two
- List the following passages on the board or on a large

piece of paper. Ask everyone to read over the portrayals of Temptation personified in Proverbs 2:16; 5:3; 5:20; 7:5; 22:14; 23:27.
- On the chalkboard or on a large piece of paper write:
—loose woman = (literally) a female stranger
—adulteress = (literally) a foreign woman
—5:3 = 5:10a and 5:10b = 5:20b
- Ask class members to turn to Proverbs 5. Point out that the word *strangers* in 5:10a is the same root word in Hebrew as the word translated *loose* in 5:3 and that the word translated *alien* in 5:10b is the same root word in Hebrew as the word translated *adulteress* in 5:20b.
- All these examples are taken from the New Revised Standard Version (NRSV), but the New International Version (NIV) does something very similar. If a King James Version (KJV) is available you will be able to see that this version has more correctly translated the words in both 5:3 and 5:20 as *strange woman*.
- Now reread all the passages listed in Part Two aloud, substituting the words *foreign woman* in each place that your translators have inserted the idea of sexual promiscuity.
- Someone will probably ask, so here is an answer in advance: In 7:10 the woman who brazenly solicits the young man's favors is called a "prostitute," which is a completely different Hebrew word than either of the words meaning foreign woman. In 23:27a the word translated *prostitute* means precisely that, but the word translated *adulteress* in 23:27b means "foreign woman." Here the two terms are parallel, implying that one is as bad as the other. This still does not justify translating "foreigner" as "adulteress" (or as NIV puts it "a wayward wife"). What the translators have done is called a modern "gloss." They have looked at what the woman in these passages seems to do (to tempt the wisdom student away from the wisdom way, to tempt the wisdom student to be unfaithful to Wisdom). Then the translators have assumed that this temptation is primarily one of sexual infidelity, and they have inserted this assumption into their renditions of the text. But it is much more likely that the wisdom pupils are being urged to resist the temptation of Foreignness (non-Israelite ways, not worshiping the Lord, or not being faithful to the Lord's wisdom). The woman portrayed in all these verses is Temptation personified (much like Folly personified in 9:13-18).
- Now that you have looked at these various ways in which women are portrayed in Proverbs, discuss some of the following questions:
—Do you see a distinct difference between the portrayals of women in Proverbs 1–9 and in Proverbs 31? between the portrayal of women in the sentence proverbs and in Proverbs 31? If so, what is the difference?
—What do you think the language used in Proverbs implies about the roles women played in the world in which the wisdom teachers lived?
—What do you think the language implies about the nature of the audience addressed by the wisdom teachers? (Does it seem like most of this was addressed to young males?)
—Are these portrayals of women descriptive or prescriptive? Do they *describe* the way things *were / are* or do they *prescribe* the way things *should be*?
—Is there any indication here that God either approves or commands women today to act like the woman in Proverbs 31? If so, who? If not, why not?
—Are these texts timely (limited in relevance to a particular place and time) or timeless (relevant in all times and in all places)?
- To close, ask people to reflect briefly and prayerfully on the wisdom and insight they have gained from studying the words of the wise in Israel.

(I) Consider the relationship between wisdom in Israel and wisdom in other countries.

- Read the "Additional Bible Helps" on page 52, and prepare to summarize or present some of the information about ancient Near Eastern wisdom literature to your class.

Part One
- Begin by asking people to look at Proverbs 22–23. Ask them to find a verse that seems to say approximately the same as the verse you are going to read to them. Then read each of the following sayings aloud, pausing after each one to see if they can match it.
—"Man is clay and straw, And the god is his builder" (see Proverbs 22:2).
—Guard against robbing the oppressed and against pushing the disabled down (see Proverbs 22:22).
—Do not associate with the hot-tempered man, nor visit him for conversation (see Proverbs 22:24).
—Don't put your heart into the pursuit of riches. . . . They will make themselves wings like geese and fly away to the heavens (Proverbs 23:4-5).
—"Do not carry off the landmark at the boundaries of the arable land . . . Nor encroach upon the boundaries of a widow. . . . [For] one satisfies god with the will of the Lord, Who determines the boundaries of the arable land" (see Proverbs 22:28 and 23:10-11).
- Then tell people that all of the above are taken from the Egyptian Instruction of Amenemope (ah-men-EM-oh-pee). Other sayings in Amenemope's writings that resemble passages in Proverbs include: "Better is bread, when the heart is happy, Than riches with sorrow" (see Proverbs 15:16-17); and "Do not lean on the scales nor falsify the weights, Nor damage the fractions of the measure. . . . Make not for thyself weights which are deficient; They abound in grief through the will of god" (see Proverbs 16:11).

You can read English versions of these and other sayings of Amenemope for yourself in *Ancient Near Eastern*

Texts Related to the Old Testament, edited by James B. Pritchard (Princeton Univ. Press; 1955; pages 421–424).

Part Two
- Present further information taken from the "Additional Bible Helps," and then discuss:
—What are some various ways to account for these kinds of similarities between Israelite and other wisdom writings?
—How does seeing similarities between Israel and its neighbors in the ancient world affect your understanding and use of the biblical texts?
- Close with a prayer addressed to the Lord, the God of Every Nation.

Additional Bible Helps

International Wisdom

The people of Israel shared certain customs, worldviews, and forms of expression with surrounding nations. Israel's own history reminds us of the many cultural and family ties that existed between Israel and the peoples of Mesopotamia and Egypt. The biblical texts themselves trace Abraham's ancestry back to Mesopotamia, and his closest relatives are said to have remained there. Abraham's first son (Ishmael) had an Egyptian mother and wife, Moses was raised in a royal Egyptian household, and Solomon had wives from all over the Middle East. Thus we ought not to be surprised to find that Israel's wisdom literature has much in common with the wisdom traditions of Egypt and Mesopotamia (including Sumer, Babylonia, and Assyria).

Like wisdom literature in Israel, Egyptian and Mesopotamian wisdom texts can be divided into "conservative" traditions, promoting the status quo (like Proverbs) and "skeptical" traditions that question traditional teachings (like Job and Ecclesiastes). A number of conservative wisdom-teaching documents (known as "Instructions") have survived to the present day. Most wisdom instructions contain very practical advice directed toward youths who aspire to hold positions of power at court. Perhaps the best-known of these is the Egyptian "Instruction of Amenemope (ah-men-EM-oh-pee)" (also spelled Amenemopet [ah-men-EM-oh-pet]), which bears an extremely close resemblance to Proverbs 22:17–24:22. The speaker in this Instruction is said to be a royal official who is trying to teach his youngest son how to succeed in the same profession. Amenemope's advice has moral and religious overtones. He says, "One thing are the words which men say, Another is that which the god does," and "Do not accept the bribe of a powerful man, Nor oppress for him the disabled. . . . justice [is] the great reward of god" (*Ancient Near Eastern Texts*, page 424).

In the category of "skeptical" texts we can list an Egyptian composition called "A Dispute Over Suicide" and a Sumerian essay called "Man and His God," which have many characteristics in common with the Book of Job, and a Babylonian text called the "Counsels of a Pessimist," which is reminiscent of Ecclesiastes. A text known as the "Babylonian Theodicy" is written in the form of a debate between a sufferer who complains (like Job does) that the wicked prosper while his piety brings him no benefits and a traditionalist who insists (as Job's friends do) that good behavior is rewarded and bad behavior is punished in this life.

Some similarities between the proverbs of Israel, Egypt, and Mesopotamia simply reflect the existence of similar worldviews and similar cultural practices. Thus, for instance, Assyrian, Egyptian, and Israelite proverbs all advise teachers and parents to speed up the process of education through the use of the "rod" or the whip. Among the documents found on the island of Elephantine is a text known as the "Words of Ahiqar" who was said to have been a wisdom teacher in the royal courts of Assyria. Ahiqar says, "Withhold not thy son from the rod, else thou wilt not be able to save him from wickedness" (*Ancient Near Eastern Texts*, page 428).

The power of the tongue (human speech) is a favored topic in the wisdom texts of Egypt, Mesopotamia, and Israel, as is the value of silence. Gossip or slander is equally despised in every culture. Such retributive sayings as "He who digs a pit will fall into it" can be found in the Egyptian Instructions of Onchsheshonqy as well as in Ecclesiastes 10:8 and Proverbs 26:27.

Egyptian myths referring to the "weighing of the human heart" after death (only the "light-hearted" went on to a life after death) may have influenced biblical sayings such as Proverbs 21:2 or 16:2, but Egyptian and Mesopotamian sayings promoting the welfare of widows and orphans are older than the origins of Israel. Babylonian wisdom texts can be traced back as far as the Sumerian (soo-MAIHR-ee-uhn) culture, which flourished around 3000 B.C. Amenemope's advice to his son ("Do not carry off the landmark . . . nor encroach upon the boundaries of a widow") had a long history in Near Eastern tradition before it found its way into Israelite texts.

The historians of Israel were familiar enough with the wisdom of other lands to be able to claim that "Solomon's wisdom surpassed the wisdom of all the people of the east, and all the wisdom of Egypt" (1 Kings 4:30). And the parallels between the words of Amenemope and the "thirty sayings" in Proverbs seem to indicate that one of the authors was familiar with (and admired) the work of the other.

But taken as a whole, Israel's wisdom literature stands out rather clearly against the international background in which it is set. While Egyptian and Mesopotamian wisdom did not distinguish between secular and religious truths, the most frequently considered topics in the biblical proverbs are good and evil (or righteousness and wickedness). References to "righteous" far outnumber references to the wise, and the "wicked" are mentioned more often than fools. In its final form, the collected words of Israel's wise men and women are permanently framed by the conviction that "the fear of the LORD" is both the beginning and the end (goal) of wisdom study.

11

Vanity of Vanities

Ecclesiastes 1:1-3; 2–3

LEARNING MENU
Keeping in mind the ways your class members learn best, as well as their needs and interests, choose at least one learning segment from each of the three Dimensions.

Advance Preparation
Three of the options for this lesson ("C," "F," and "G") suggest using fairly well-known songs from the mid-1960's as discussion-starters for various parts of Ecclesiastes. These two songs are: "Turn! Turn! Turn!" ("To Everything There Is a Season"; adaptation and music by Pete Seeger, recorded by the Byrds. Columbia Records released this hit song in 1965) and "Richard Cory" ("Sounds of Silence" album; written by Paul Simon, 1965 Young Music Ltd., London, England).

If you choose any of these options, be sure to gather all the equipment needed (such as a record, tape or CD, and player). Check for electrical outlets or if you will need an extension cord or batteries to operate your player. If you can get the lyrics or sheet music instead of a recording, you might be able to get one or two of your class members to sing for the class. Be sure to ask them ahead of time.

Dimension 1: What Does the Bible Say?

(A) Hold a time of opening worship.

- You may choose to begin today's session by singing together "All Things Bright and Beautiful" (*The United Methodist Hymnal*, 147). This hymn is not based on an Ecclesiastes text. However, it is a praise hymn with a creation focus.

(B) Share answers to the Dimension 1 questions in the study book.

- Discussion of the questions may lead in these directions:
  1. Encourage class members not merely to quote the text but to use their own words and terms to describe what they think the speaker was doing in Ecclesiastes 2:1-11.
  2. There are a variety of possible answers people could give to the second question. Be sure that everyone has at least noticed the reasons for despair given in 2:18-21.
  3. Again, encourage people to phrase their answers in their own words rather than in quotations from the text.
  4. There are several possible answers to this question as well. Be sure that people have at least noted 2:24-26, 3:10-11, and 3:13-14.

(C) Listen to musical versions of Ecclesiastes 3.

- One of the "Golden Oldies" from the mid 1960's is a song based directly on Ecclesiastes 3:1-8. This song, "Turn! Turn! Turn!" ("To Everything There Is a Season"), was recorded by the Byrds in 1965. If you can get a recording or a copy of the song, ask your class members to look at the biblical text while they listen to the words of the song.
- Then discuss the following questions:
—How close is the song to your Bible translation?
—Where does the song differ?
—Why do you think the song differs in the way it does?

Dimension 2:
What Does the Bible Mean?

(D) Get clear about the meaning of vanity (*hebel*).

In every language, words have potential ranges of meaning, depending on how they are used in specific situations. Think, for instance, of the common English word *run*. We can say that animals and people *run*, but so do machines, noses, nylon stockings, politicians seeking office, and theatrical productions. Each of these ways of using the word *run* would have to be translated by a different term in Spanish, French, or Hebrew. In a similar way, Bible translators often have to use different English terms to express the meaning of a single Hebrew word when it is used in different ways.

To illustrate the potential range of meaning that the word *hebel* has in Hebrew, look at the variety of English words that have been used to translate it in different contexts.

- You will need a variety of Bible translations available in the classroom. Try to include a King James Version (KJV), a New International Version (NIV), a *New American Bible* (NAB), a *Jerusalem Bible* (JB), a *Good News Bible* (*The Bible in Today's English Version,* TEV), and a Revised Standard or New Revised Standard Version (RSV/NRSV).
- Divide class members into four groups. Write the following texts on the chalkboard or on a large piece of paper where everyone can see them. Assign one grouping of texts to each group of students.

—**Group 1:** Texts in which the word *hebel* is translated "breath" in the NRSV:
   Psalm 39:5, 11   Psalm 144:4
   Psalm 62:9

—**Group 2:** Texts in which *hebel* is translated as "vain" in the NRSV:
   Job 27:12   Lamentations 4:17
   Psalm 62:10   Jonah 2:8
   Proverbs 31:30

—**Group 3:** Texts in which *hebel* is translated "worthless" in the NRSV:
   Psalm 31:6   Jeremiah 2:5
   Isaiah 30:7   Jeremiah 10:15

—**Group 4:** Texts in which *hebel* is translated "empty" in the NRSV:
   Job 35:16   Zechariah 10:2

- Ask Group 4 also to turn to the NRSV translation of Proverbs 21:6 and guess which words are used to translate *hebel* in this saying ("fleeting vapor").
- Tell the groups to read the assigned texts in several translations and to try to determine what point is being made each time the word *hebel* is used. (It may be necessary to look at the verse right before and right after your verse to get the full sense.)
- Then paraphrase (state in your own words) each of the verses in such a way that you make clear the implications of meaning that the word *hebel* has in this context. See if you can find a synonym for the word that is used in your verses to translate *hebel*.
- When the groups have had time to complete this assignment, come back together to share your conclusions.
- Write on chalkboard or on a large piece of paper the synonyms each group has found for *hebel* from its passages.
- Invite class members to question any synonyms that they may not see as justifiable, further inviting those who came up with the synonym to explain it.
- Now go back into Ecclesiastes and examine the chapters studied in this lesson. Read the verses where *vain* and *vanity* are used in the NRSV of Ecclesiastes (2:2, 11, 15, 17, 19, 21, 23, 26; 3:19), and try out some of the substitute meanings you have derived from the other biblical contexts in which *hebel* was used.
- Ask the class whether they think Qoheleth has a unified definition for this term. Does *hebel* mean just one thing or does it have a fairly wide range of meanings when it is used in different parts of Ecclesiastes?

(E) Illustrate Qoheleth's "Test of Pleasure."

- For this activity you will need three pieces of posterboard (one for each group); art supplies (such as scissors, colored paper or felt, markers, glue); magazines, catalogs, or other publications with pictures; and a larger piece of posterboard or other large piece of paper. Read Ecclesiastes 2:4-8 to get a sense of the types of pictures your class will need for this learning option.
- Divide class members into three groups.
- Ask each group to draw or cut and glue pictorial characterizations of Qoheleth's "test of pleasure"—Ecclesiastes 2:4-8— onto its piece of posterboard. Include some or all of the acquisitions mentioned in this passage and an illustration of Qoheleth's face or body language, reflecting his feelings at different stages of the "test."
- Invite your small groups to share their Qoheleth creations.

- Using these posters, the whole class could create a large mural to display in the classroom. Sections of the actual Scripture could be printed onto the mural to explain the origin and meaning of the various pictures.

(F) Look at lyrics in their original contexts.

- You will need a large piece of posterboard or paper for this learning option. Divide this paper into two sections. You will need markers for writing.
- Recruit class members to read aloud Ecclesiastes 3:1-8, perhaps one person per verse, or two persons to read alternate verses. Present the reading.
- Ask class members to tell the times or places in which they have often heard the familiar passage in 3:1-8. It may have been at a funeral or on a sympathy card or in a song. If you were able to get a copy of the song "Turn! Turn! Turn!" play it or sing it for the class (if you have not already done so).
- As the class members discuss the following question, ask someone to make brief notes of the discussion on half of the board or paper.
—When you heard these words before in settings such as funerals, sympathy cards, or songs, what did you think they meant?
- On the other half of the board or paper ask someone to write the results of these questions:
—What do you think this text means now that you have studied it in light of its context?
—How is the point made in 3:1-8 related to the question raised in 3:9?
—How is 3:1-8 related to 3:16-17?
—Has reading this text in its context changed your understanding of its meaning?

Dimension 3: What Does the Bible Mean to Us?

(G) Compare Qoheleth's life experiences with our own.

Part One
Another song that was popular in the mid 1960's was Simon and Garfunkel's "Richard Cory" (from their "Sounds of Silence" album). The lyrics tell the story of a man who was born into a wealthy family, who had "everything money could buy." Others wished they could have a life like Richard Cory. He gave generously to others and was well thought of by the townspeople. Then he shocked everyone when he "went home last night and put a bullet through his head."
- Play the song, or tell this story for the class. Then discuss these questions:

—What do you think was Richard Cory's problem?
—Are you familiar with cases such as Richard Cory's in your own experience?
—Why do you think successful, affluent people who seem to have "reached the top" (whether it is in school, work, sports, or whatever) sometimes start questioning whether life is worth living?
—Are there any similarities between the Richard Cory story and what is said in Ecclesiastes 2:1-23?
—Does Ecclesiastes address problems that still exist in the modern world?

Part Two
- An Associated Press report printed in the *Dayton Daily News* (April 17, 1995) said that in a survey conducted by the Lutheran Brotherhood, "Seventy percent of the households interviewed said they considered their financial situation to be somewhat a reflection of God's regard for them."
—Would Ecclesiastes agree with this majority opinion or not?
—Would Job?
—Do you?
- Close by reading Luke 12:16-21 (the parable of the rich fool).

(H) Name the areas of *hebel*/vanity in your life.

By now your class has probably spent a fair amount of time researching and discussing what it is that Qoheleth means when he says "vanity/*hebel*." Now it is time to let the class explore what vanity/*hebel* means to them as individuals and/or as a group.

Part One
- Ask for a class member to take notes on the chalkboard or on a large piece of paper. Begin by having this person write "vanity/*hebel*" at the top in large letters.
- Ask class members to brainstorm things or situations in their lives that seem to them to be vanity/*hebel* as they understand the term. This could range from busywork that they have to do in their jobs, to the fancy decor of the church sanctuary.
- Let them brainstorm uninterrupted on this for a few minutes. Then, allow class members to ask questions of each other's ideas and in turn explain why they see some of these things as vanity/*hebel*.
- Emphasize that exploring ideas here is the point, not attacking them.

Part Two
- For this activity give each class member a piece of paper, and have crayons, markers, pens, and pencils available.
- Ask class members to describe, through drawing pictures or writing words, what they see as vanity/*hebel* in their lives.
- As they are finishing, ask if anyone is willing to share what he or she has created with the rest of the class.

Part Three
- Read aloud Ecclesiastes 1:3; 2:22-24.
- Discuss Ecclesiastes' challenging assertion that excessive striving or toil is *hebel*.
—What kinds of work or striving have you experienced as *hebel*?
—What kinds of work have you done that you think would fit into Ecclesiastes' category of enjoyment (as in 2:24)?
—What is it that causes toil to be *hebel* or not?
- Close by reading Luke 12:16-21 (the parable of the rich fool).

(I) Compare and contrast the opinions of Proverbs and Ecclesiastes with your own opinions.

- To prepare, read over the "Additional Bible Helps," this page, entitled "Comparing and Contrasting Proverbs and Ecclesiastes."

Part One
- Ask class members to discuss Qoheleth's basic premise in 3:1-8.
—Do you think Qoheleth is right in saying that "there is a season, and a time for every matter under heaven"?
—Do you agree that there is an appropriate time for killing (3:3), for hate, or for war (3:8)?
—These things do happen in life, but do you think these are things that have "appointed" times or seasons in life?
- Try to make this an open discussion in which people will feel free to express differing opinions without fearing condemnation from anyone. Your goal is to expose the issues, not to come to an agreement.

Part Two
- Divide a large section of your chalkboard or a large piece of paper into four parts and label each section as illustrated below:

	Work	Wisdom	Retribution
Proverbs			
Ecclesiastes			
Me / Us			
Jesus			

- Ask class members to help you fill in the chart:
—What do Ecclesiastes and the Proverbialists say you can gain with hard work?
—What do they say you can gain with wisdom?
—What do they say about justice and retribution?
—What do you think about each of these issues?
—What might Jesus say about these issues?
- To close with this learning option, read the parable of the laborers in the vineyard, Matthew 20:1-16.

(J) Think about what "season" you are in now.

The following questions are discussion starters. As always feel free to add your own ideas.
- Give class members some quiet time, paper and pencil or pen. Ask them to reflect for a few minutes and to jot down what "time" it seems to be in their lives right now.
- Think about what is going on in your own community or nation.
—Does this seem to be a time that fits into any of the categories in 3:1-8?
—What makes you think so?
—Does the fact that something is currently happening mean that it is necessarily the "right" time or appropriate time from God's point of view?
- Think about what is going on in your own church.
—Does it seem to be an appropriate time for your church to be built up (3:3)?
—Is it an appropriate time for the church to be silent (3:7)?
—How can the church know or find out "what time it is" according to God's plans?
- Think about what is going on in your personal, professional, or faith life.
—What "time" does it seem to be in your life right now?
—Does this present time in your life seem to you to be a part of God's overall plan or out of season or out of sync with God's plans?
- To close, offer these personal reflections up to God in silent prayer.

Additional Bible Helps

Comparing and Contrasting Proverbs and Ecclesiastes
There are a number of areas in which the books of Proverbs and Ecclesiastes agree. Qoheleth (the speaker in the Book of Ecclesiastes) seems to say that almost any kind of behavior can be justified under the right circumstances. It is the timing of an action that matters (Ecclesiastes 3:1-8). Even war and hate can be appropriate in certain contexts. This seems to be similar to the attitude of the collectors of Proverbs who put the sayings in Proverbs 26:4 and 26:5 one right after the other. By setting these contrary statements down next to each other in Proverbs, the collectors imply that a given action can be either right or wrong, depending on what else is going on at the time when it is done.

There is also an essential agreement between Proverbs 13:23 (which is a minority viewpoint in the Book of Proverbs) and Ecclesiastes 5:8-9. Both books recognize that injustice is sometimes perpetrated by the very officials to whom the responsibility for promoting justice is entrusted.

Like Proverbs 10:8, 12:15, and 13:10, Ecclesiastes 4:13 agrees that the wise are willing to listen to the advice of others. The wisdom of many is superior to the wisdom of one (Proverbs 11:14; 15:22).

However, there are also a number of distinct differences between these two "companion volumes" of wisdom literature. In Proverbs, hard work is always admired and laziness is always condemned (see 12:24). But Ecclesiastes points out that there is folly in pursuing either extreme (Ecclesiastes 4:5-6 and 7:16-18). Ecclesiastes challenges people to evaluate the goals or purposes that motivate them to work hard. He suggests that much of the hard work we do is based on greed or aimed at "keeping up with the Joneses" (4:4, 8). Ecclesiastes points out that working hard in order to accumulate more possessions is folly, because wealth is inherently unable to satisfy us (5:10, 6:7). The more your goods increase so do those who consume them, and it gets harder and harder to sleep at night (5:11-12; see 2:23). And everyone knows that you cannot take it with you when you die (5:13-15)!

While both Proverbs and Ecclesiastes value wisdom highly, Proverbs makes some extravagant claims, asserting that wisdom leads to "life" (Proverbs 3:18). While Ecclesiastes is willing to concede that wisdom may help the wise avoid some dangers, and thus stay alive longer (2:14a, 7:12), he points out that the same "fate" (death) eventually awaits both the foolish and the wise (Ecclesiastes 2:14b-16). Proverbs optimistically assumes that human beings possess everything they need to discover truth, if only they will look to the right sources and work hard at attaining wisdom. But Ecclesiastes thinks God has imposed definite limits on human reason (3:11; 8:17). Qoheleth says there are many things we cannot know and cannot find out (3:21-22; 6:12; 7:14; 8:17 11:5).

In Proverbs "Fear of the LORD" is virtually equated with the acquisition of wisdom (for example 1:7, 29; 2:1-5). But in Ecclesiastes, the fear of God is linked with our *inability* to know or to change whatever God has done "from the beginning to the end" (3:11-14). It is the fact that we do not know and cannot know what God has done, is doing, or will do that causes us to hold God in awe or reverence. Thus, the one who fears God will avoid extremes, knowing that the future cannot be known (7:13-18).

The speakers in Proverbs (like the Deuteronomic historians who produced Joshua through Second Kings) often imply that God's judgment will give tangible, material rewards and punishments to people in this life, under the sun (Proverbs 3:9-10, 11:8, and others). But Qoheleth concludes that there is no positive correlation between moral behavior and prosperity or between immoral behavior and poverty (Ecclesiastes 9:11-12). Retributive theology fails to explain the realities of human experience (Ecclesiastes 3:16-22 and 8:10-14).

Qoheleth is willing to believe the faith claim that God will bring everything into judgment (12:14), as long as he is not asked to think that judgment will take place "under the sun." If it is true, as Ecclesiastes claims, that God has appointed a time for every matter (3:17), then God has probably appointed a time for judging the bad and the good. But the critical observation of human experience tells us that this time is not "under the sun." Under the sun it is clear to Qoheleth that justice is not always done (3:16; 4:1; 7:15; 8:14; 9:11).

The differences that predominate between Proverbs and Ecclesiastes may grow out of differences in life experience. Most of the speakers in Proverbs seem to have lived in a stable, orderly, and mostly predictable society. Their cherished beliefs both grew out of daily life experiences in such a society and were reinforced by these experiences. They were aware of the possibility that their best-laid plans might be diverted by God's purposes (19:21; 21:30-31), but for the most part their lives followed an orderly and relatively predictable pattern.

Ecclesiastes speaks in the midst of turbulent times, when the old order is rapidly changing. The consequences that follow actions in the new order no longer seem even remotely predictable.

12
Ecclesiastes 8:10–9:12; 11–12

THE POWER OF POSITIVE PESSIMISM

LEARNING MENU
Keeping in mind the ways your class members learn best, as well as their needs and interests, choose at least one learning segment from each of the three Dimensions.

Dimension 1:
What Does the Bible Say?

(A) Open with worship.

- A suggested opening worship time is to sing or read aloud "Breathe on Me, Breath of God," *The United Methodist Hymnal*, 420.

(B) Answer the Dimension 1 questions in the study book.

- Discussion of the questions may lead in these directions:
  1. Encourage people to use their own words to describe what is said to be "vanity" in 8:10-17. The essential problem being described in this section is the fact that the wicked do not seem to be punished in this life either by society or by God.
  2. As people share their answers to this question, encourage them to give the chapter and verse location where they found each item. Look at the chart illustrating the organization of the Book of Ecclesiastes (inside back cover of the study book), and check off the verses that people identify under the heading on the chart entitled "But We Can't Know."
  3. Answers to this question may vary considerably, depending on which Bible translation persons used in their reading. Many people have understood 11:1 as a reference to charity; but *The Good News Bible* (*The Bible in Today's English Version*, TEV) makes it sound like financial investment advice, and the study book suggests it refers to sowing seed while the ground is still wet. Some readers think 11:4 encourages people to pay attention to weather signs and to refrain from sowing or reaping when it looks like rain. Others (including the study book) see this as a warning *not* to refrain from sowing and reaping just because the weather is uncertain.
  4. Point out that the conclusion that an editor has contributed to Ecclesiastes comes from the observation that 12:9-10 speaks in the third person *about* Qoheleth. After people have had a chance to share the answers they gave to this question, ask them whether they think the editor approved of Qoheleth.

(C) Explore what Ecclesiastes says we do not know.

- Write the following verse numbers on small pieces of paper (one passage per piece of paper): Ecclesiastes 8:6-7; 8:17; 9:1; 9:5; 9:12; 10:14; 11:2; 11:5; 11:6.
- Put the pieces in a bowl, box, or hat; ask participants to draw one out.
- Give people a minute to look up their verse or verses in Ecclesiastes, then have them read aloud in random order.
- Briefly discuss these questions:
—What do all of these passages have in common?
—Has there been a distinct change in what we know since Qoheleth's time?
—Do we now have answers for any of the things Qoheleth said we could not know?

(D) Picture the "days of trouble."

- For this activity you will need drawing materials, such as paper, pencils, crayons, and markers.
- Also you will need these Bible translations: New International Version (NIV), Revised Standard Version (RSV), and New Revised Standard Version (NRSV).
- Divide class members into five groups.
- Assign one verse in Ecclesiastes 12:2-6 to each group.
- Give each group paper and drawing materials. Ask them to illustrate the *literal* pictures implied in their assigned verse.
- Tell them to leave the interpretation of their picture until later. (In other words, draw a tree in blossom for verse 5.) These drawings could be done as individual-sized posters (with either one designated "artist" per group or with each person in the group sketching his or her idea as a part of the whole). Or the sketches could be done in the form of a large mural drawn on a long strip of paper.
- If you use this option, a good follow-up with a discussion of the meanings of the literal pictures is option "G."

Dimension 2: What Does the Bible Mean?

(E) Look for reasons to recommend enjoyment.

- Be sure to read the "Additional Bible Helps" found on page 62 of this leader's guide.

Part One
- Ask people how they feel about what they have been reading in Ecclesiastes.
—Is Ecclesiastes a gloomy book?
—Have you felt depressed by the readings, or have you felt liberated, freed, or uplifted? Why, or why not?
—What has Qoheleth said that seems most memorable?
—What specific things stick out in your mind from what you have read?

Part Two
- Using the information in the "Additional Bible Helps" (page 62), list on the chalkboard or on a large piece of paper the passages in which Qoheleth recommends enjoyment.
- Assign each passage to a small group.
- Ask each group to read its passage and to determine what the problem is that Qoheleth has identified just before he makes his recommendation for enjoyment.
- Ask each group to report back to the whole class, summarizing the problem and reading what Qoheleth says we should do about it.
- Write the reasons next to the verse citations on the chalkboard or large piece of paper.

(F) Compare what Proverbs and Ecclesiastes say about justice, rewards, and punishments.

Choose this option only if you did not get a chance to compare Proverbs and Ecclesiastes in last week's class session. Read or review the "Additional Bible Helps" in Chapter 11, page 56.

- Divide your chalkboard into two parts or use two pieces of paper. Write "Proverbs" at the top of one and "Ecclesiastes" at the top of the other.
- Divide class members into four groups.
- Ask two of the groups to look for passages in Proverbs that say something about the consequences of right and wrong actions.
- Ask the other two groups to look for passages in Ecclesiastes that say something about the consequences of right and wrong actions.

The two Ecclesiastes groups should be able to find statements that challenge the prevailing opinion in Proverbs. Some of these passages are: Ecclesiastes 3:16; 4:1; 7:15; 8:10-11; 8:14; and 9:2. Some of the passages that agree with the dominant point of view in Proverbs are: Ecclesiastes 3:17; 8:12-13; 11:9; 12:4.

Scripture suggestions for the Proverbs groups are some of the following: Proverbs 10:2, 3, 29; 12:7; 13:21; 14:32; 26:27; 28:10; 29:6. Be sure they have discovered Proverbs 22:8 ("One who sows injustice will reap calamity") as well as 22:9, 16, 22.

(G) Find new meanings in the pictures in 12:2-6.

This option is suggested as a follow-up to "D."
- You will need to have several versions of the Bible for this activity: RSV, NRSV, NIV, *Good News Bible*

THE POWER OF POSITIVE PESSIMISM

(TEV), others. You will also need a marker and large piece of paper or chalk and a chalkboard.
- Read each verse aloud from an RSV, NRSV, or NIV Bible. As class members brainstorm some of the possible meanings, write these ideas on your chalkboard or large piece of paper.
- Then have someone read the *Good News Bible*'s version of these verses aloud to the class. Discuss with your class:
—What difference does it make to hear this passage in figuratively stated picture-language as opposed to the stark reality of the *Good News* version?
- Now go back to the drawing board—your groupings for option "D." This time ask them to try to sketch what the *meaning* that lies behind the literal pictures seems to be.
- Place these new interpretive drawings beneath or in the near vicinity of your original drawings.
- Mark both sets of sketches with the appropriate chapter and verse numbers in Ecclesiastes.
- Continue this discussion by using option "K."

(H) Illustrate what we do not know.

- You will need markers and posterboard or a large piece of paper for this option.
- Ask class members to work together on a "poster" that will sum up Qoheleth's belief that we simply do not know much about the past, the present, or the future.
- Choose one class member to be the poster-maker.
- Ask other class members to look through Ecclesiastes (especially this week's reading) for words and phrases that describe Qoheleth's "thesis" of not knowing.
- These should then be written on the poster in collage-style by the poster-maker.
- For example: "They do not know what is to be" (8:7); "The living know that they will die, but the dead know nothing" (9:5); "No one can anticipate the time of disaster" (9:12); "You do not know the work of God" (11:5).
- This poster can remain in your classroom as a reminder of your study of Qoheleth.

Dimension 3:
What Does the Bible Mean to Us?

(I) Weigh and evaluate Qoheleth's conclusions.

This option can be used as a follow-up for either option "E" or "F."

Tell class members: "Just as Qoheleth weighed and evaluated the reliability of the traditional sayings handed down to him, using his own reason, life experiences, and observations as a measuring stick, so also must we weigh and evaluate Qoheleth's truth claims according to our own standards of judgment."

Part One
- Evaluate the reasons Qoheleth gives for recommending enjoyment.
- Ask people if the following claims are true in their experience:
—The results of human work are not permanent.
—The results of your work have to be left to others when you die.
—There is no ultimate satisfaction in working simply to pile up possessions.
—The fate of humans and the fate of animals is the same, as one dies so dies the other . . . all are from the dust, and all turn to dust again.
—The righteous are sometimes treated like the wicked and the wicked are sometimes treated like the righteous.
—The same fate comes to all.
- Then discuss these questions:
—Is the solution Qoheleth offers to all these problems (to enjoy what we have while we have it) satisfactory? Why or why not?
—Is there an alternative way to answer these problems that Qoheleth pinpoints from his experience? If so, suggest a way.

Part Two
- Evaluate what Qoheleth says about justice:

Advance Preparation
If you choose this option, you will want to go back and reread the article on "Theodicy" from the "Additional Bible Helps" in Chapter 2 (page 12).

- Ask the class members to break into pairs.
- Ask the pairs to focus on Ecclesiastes 8:14: ". . . there are righteous people who are treated according to the conduct of the wicked, and there are wicked people who are treated according to the conduct of the righteous."
- Then ask them to think of situations in which they have seen one (the righteous treated according to the conduct of the wicked) or the other (the wicked treated according to the conduct of the righteous) happen and describe them to each other.
- Assure class members that these can, but need not be, personal situations.
- Following these one-on-one discussion sessions, call the whole class back together and discuss:
—What sense might be made of these real situations (which they may or may not choose to share with the rest of the class)?
—Why is it the case that "there are righteous people who are treated according to the conduct of the wicked" (8:14) and vice versa? What causes or allows this to happen?
- Write some of the ideas people come up with on the chalkboard or on a large piece of paper.

Be prepared to encounter and facilitate various theological views.

For example, someone might say that it is better for us to have free will than for God to intervene in our lives, even to prevent bad things from happening. This might go on the chalkboard or on the paper simply as "free will."

Someone might say that God simply does not choose to work in such a way as to intervene and change things.

Or that God is "not powerful enough" to enforce retributive theology.

Someone might rest on the Qoheleth-like thought that the world does not seem to work according to retributive theology, and we do not and cannot know why this is.

Some class members may simply reject the question, as Job's friends did, asserting that bad things do not happen to good people and vice versa. (This argument assumes that the things we see as bad are not really bad; they are really good and we just cannot see why.)

Insist that this discussion must be open and accepting of different opinions. The rule of the day is to offer the pros and cons of an answer to the retributive theology question. While it may upset the sensibilities of some to see "God is not all-powerful" or "God needs to test us" on the board or paper, considering these same options could be quite helpful to others.

- When this discussion has had some time in which to take on a life of its own and the class time is nearing a close, gather class members in a circle for a closing prayer in which you ask for patience and wisdom in the quest to understand.

(J) Summarize your learnings.

- Your class has spent five sessions studying Proverbs and Ecclesiastes.
- Ask students to divide into pairs and to discuss their final impressions of this body of literature.
—For instance, when they think of Proverbs and Ecclesiastes in the future, what will come to mind?
—What are some words that characterize these books?
—What sets these books apart as unique or memorable in the students' minds?
—If they had to explain Proverbs and Ecclesiastes to a second- or third-grader, what would they say?
- When the pairs have had a chance to go through these questions, recruit someone to be the class writer.
- The title at the top of the chalkboard or large piece of paper should simply read, "Proverbs and Ecclesiastes."
- Ask the pairs to share some of the words, descriptions, and impressions that they came up with.
- These ideas can then be written down by the class writer in a collage fashion. If this is done on a large sheet of paper, it could help to post it on the wall of the classroom, so that the class might remember their work on these books as they go on to study other parts of the Bible.

(K) Look at how we talk about death.

- Use this option to follow-up your attempts to picture what is said in Ecclesiastes 12:1-6 in options "D" and "G."
- Tell class members: "We can sometimes tell what people think and feel about aging and death by listening to the words they use to describe (or to avoid describing) these realities in our lives."
- Write "Aging" on one side and "Death" on the other side of your chalkboard or large sheet of paper, and list the words and phrases as people suggest them.
- Ask people to name euphemisms for aging and death that they have heard or used (ways of talking about aging and death without actually using either of those words).
- Discuss these questions:
—Why do we use these roundabout ways of speaking?
—What does each of these terms imply about the sensitivities, beliefs, or fears people have about aging and death?
—Why do you think Ecclesiastes 12:1-6 talks about aging and death in the way it does?
—Is Ecclesiastes 12:1-6 a depressing or a liberating (freeing) passage to read or to hear?
—Do Christian beliefs fit or not fit into Qoheleth's picture? Why, or why not?
- Close with a moment of silent prayer.

(L) Stand up for what you think you know.

Qoheleth concludes that he just does not know what to think about the nature of God's justice or about how the world actually works. That's just fine for Qoheleth, but what do the members of your class think? Do they think they understand the way that God and the world work or not?

- Set up a continuum across the classroom space. Identify one end of the room as "know" and the other as "don't know," and remind class members that this knowing has to do with knowledge about God and the way God works in the world.
- Ask class members to line up along the continuum according to how close they feel they are to knowing or not knowing.
- Let class members examine one another's location on the continuum, and then ask them to take their seats again for discussion.
—First, ask them to reflect on their overall distribution.
—Where were most of the people standing?
—Were they evenly spread out on the continuum?
—Were they all bunched up in one place?
—Did most people tend toward one end or the other?
- Then ask people to share their individual reasons for choosing their places along the continuum. If you think the class members might be hesitant to discuss this within the larger group, ask them to split into pairs to discuss this and the following questions:

—Are Qoheleth's assertions that we do not know convincing to you?
—Do you think knowing is related to having faith? Why, or why not?
• Following this discussion, ask one of the class members to offer a closing prayer.

Additional Bible Helps

Qoheleth's Life Orientation

The speaker in Ecclesiastes has been wrongly accused of having a gloomy outlook on life. In part, this is due to the traditional translation of his thematic statement (which really means "A breath of a breath. Everything is a breath"). And in part it is because Qoheleth's "reality therapy" seems overly pessimistic to those who have been comfortably ignoring the realities of human existence. But in fact, Qoheleth is realistic rather than pessimistic about life and its possibilities for enjoyment. Readers who get bogged down in Ecclesiastes' negative statements may fail to notice how often these negative conclusions are turned into reasons for enjoying life as it really is.

Over and over again, Qoheleth commends enjoyment of the simplest things in life. The power of enjoyment is the only thing we own that is truly our own and cannot be taken away from us. Everything else we gain from our toil must be passed on to another when we die (6:2).

In the Jewish liturgical tradition, the Book of Ecclesiastes is read in its entirety during the autumn festival known as *Sukkoth* (SUHK-uhth, translated "Booths" or "Tabernacles"). The name of the festival refers to a kind of temporary shelter, the kind that was used by the people of Israel as they wandered in the wilderness on their way to the Promised Land and the kind that was later set up in the fields during the time of harvest after they had settled in and grown crops on that Promised Land.

Sukkoth is a festival of joy, but it has a double purpose. On the one hand, it is a harvest festival: a time for people to celebrate the bounty of the agricultural year (Deuteronomy 16:13-15). On the other hand, it is a time for people to remember when they had no homes, no crops, no harvests (Leviticus 23:33-44).

In the wilderness, Israel depended on God alone for sustenance. Manna was provided day by day, just enough for everyone to be satisfied but never enough for anyone to stockpile or hoard. Those "who gathered much had nothing over, and those who gathered little had no shortage; they gathered as much as each of them needed" (Exodus 16:18). Anything that was left over quickly spoiled.

But once the people of God began to reap the harvests of the Promised Land, they were tempted to forget that it was God who made the harvest possible. So the festival of Sukkoth functioned as a reminder to the people of God that they were as dependent on God for sustenance in the Promised Land as they were in their wilderness wanderings. And when the Book of Ecclesiastes is read at Sukkoth, it reminds the people of God that their material abundance is as transitory as a "breath" of air. Like manna, the fruits of our labors are gifts from God to be used and enjoyed, not hoarded.

Jesus was said to have participated in Sukkoth (John 7:1-39), and Christians might be well-advised to follow his example. Whenever we count our blessings, whenever we rejoice in a successful venture, we need to remember what Ecclesiastes tells us. Possessions, wisdom, power, health, loved ones, and even life itself are all *hebel*, a breath, lacking in permanence but not in worth. This, however, is not a cause for despair but a reason for us to enjoy the gifts of God in the present age.

Qoleleth's Reasons for Enjoying Life

1. Even though the results of your work are not permanent and you cannot take your material possessions with you when you die . . . you can eat, drink, and find enjoyment (NIV says "satisfaction") in your work (2:24).

2. Even though you cannot know what the future holds for you . . . you can be happy and enjoy yourself as long as you live (3:11-12).

3. Even though there is wickedness in the world, and no real evidence that God will reward the righteous or punish the wicked . . . you still should enjoy your work, for that is your "lot" (3:22).

4. Even though there is no ultimate satisfaction to be gained from wealth, . . . it is nevertheless "fitting" for us to eat and drink and find enjoyment in all the work we do under the sun (5:18).

5. Even though wealth is easily lost, even though we leave life as naked as we come into it (5:13-16), nevertheless . . . God gives us the ability to be happy in our work and in our possessions while we have them (5:19).

6. Even though the righteous are sometimes treated like the wicked and the wicked are sometimes treated as though they were righteous . . . I commend enjoyment, . . . for this will go with you in your toil through the days of life that God gives you under the sun (8:15).

7. Even though the same fate comes to all . . . "go eat your bread with enjoyment, and drink your wine with a merry heart; for God has long ago approved what you do" (9:7).

8. Even though "there is no work or thought or knowledge or wisdom in Sheol, to which you are going" (9:10) . . . wear the nicest clothes you own, enjoy life with the spouse that you love, and "whatever your hand finds to do, do with your might" (9:8-10).

9. Even though the days of darkness will be many . . . rejoice while you are young, and "let your heart cheer you in the days of your youth" (11:9).

13
Song of Solomon 1–2; 4–5; 8

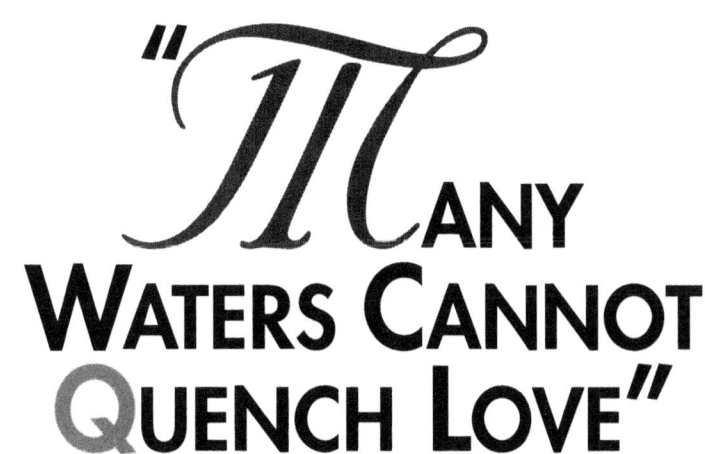

"Many Waters Cannot Quench Love"

LEARNING MENU
Keeping in mind the ways your class members learn best, as well as their needs and interests, choose at least one learning segment from each of the three Dimensions.

Dimension 1: What Does the Bible Say?

(A) Hold an opening worship time.

- The following responsive reading is found in *The United Methodist Hymnal* (646). You may choose to use hymnals and have everyone read or have two people read responsively.

> Let love be genuine and live in harmony;
>   hate what is evil, hold fast to what is good.
>   Outdo one another in showing honor;
>   be humble and never conceited.
> **Love is stronger than death**
>   **and jealousy is cruel as the grave.**
>   **Floods cannot drown love**
>   **and wealth cannot buy it.**

(B) Answer the Dimension 1 questions in the study book.

- Discussion of the Dimension 1 questions may lead in these directions:
  1. Ask people to say *why* they thought what they did about the season portrayed in the first two chapters. (The Song of Solomon is traditionally associated with spring [2:11-15], the time in which plants are bursting into bloom and the vineyards [as well as lovers] are "in blossom.")
  2. The answers you get to this question may range from "not much" to the naming of one or two figures of speech that still communicate in our own culture (such as "better is your love than wine" in 4:10).
  3. Since the metaphors are very mixed (from our way of looking at them) you may get a wide variety of answers here as well.
  4. It seems that the woman would like to be able to show her love in open and public ways, as she could do with her brother but cannot do with her lover.

(C) Read the text aloud.

Advance Preparation

As class members are gathering and before class time begins, recruit a woman and a man to read aloud Chapter 1 in the Song of Solomon. Using the chart that illustrates the distribution of voices found in the study book (page 106), divide up and mark the speaking parts. Ask the woman to read the female voice and the man to read the male voice. (Give them a few minutes to get clear on where their parts change.)

If you wish, you can also assign the second half of verse 4 and verse 11 to a chorus of two or more voices. Some readers think the *we* refers to a chorus; others think that the lovers use *we* when they speak about themselves in these verses.

- Ask your recruits to read Chapter 1 aloud to the class. Then ask class members to comment on what difference it makes in their perception of the material to hear it in this dialogue form.
- If you think class members would be comfortable doing so, you might want to do the same with some of the other material assigned for today's reading. But be sensitive to the fact that some people will feel too embarrassed to read some of this material out loud in front of others.

Dimension 2: What Does the Bible Mean?

(D) Look carefully at Song of Solomon 8:6-7.

- Before class begins you will need to gather several different Bible translations. Try to include a King James Version (KJV), a New International Version (NIV), a *New American Bible* (NAB), a *Jerusalem Bible* (JB), a *Good News Bible* (TEV), and a Revised Standard or New Revised Standard Version (RSV/NRSV).
- Begin your examination of these verses by reading them aloud in one version and having people note where other translations differ from the one that is read.
- Refer to the chart below for ways of translating Song of Solomon 8:6b-7a:

NIV: "For love is as strong as death,
its jealousy unyielding as the grave.
It burns like blazing fire,
like a mighty flame.
Many waters cannot quench love;
rivers cannot wash it away."

NAB: "For stern as death is love,
relentless as the nether world is devotion
its flames are a blazing fire.
Deep waters cannot quench love,
nor floods sweep it away."

NRSV: "For love is strong as death,
passion fierce as the grave.
Its flashes are flashes of fire,
a raging flame.
Many waters cannot quench love,
neither can floods drown it."

TEV: "Love is as powerful as death;
passion is as strong as death itself.
It bursts into flame
and burns like a raging fire.
Water cannot put it out;
no flood can drown it."

Point out that the word that is translated "grave" in many of these translations is the Hebrew word *sheol*. (See "Popular Theology in Wisdom Literature and Psalms," page 70.)

- Point out that in Hebrew the terms that are here translated "many waters" and "floods/rivers" echo the ancient Near Eastern creation stories in which the creator God is forced to subdue chaotic watery powers before bringing the created order into being.
- After comparing translations, discuss these questions:
—What is compared to what in these verses?
—How is the metaphor in the first two lines of verse 7 related to the metaphor in the last two lines of verse 6?
—What is the point made by these metaphors?
- Continue this discussion by using option "H."

(E) Compare three passages.

- Ask class members to read Song of Solomon 8:6-7, Ecclesiastes 12:1-8, and Psalm 73:21-28, looking for likenesses and differences.
- After they have had time to do the reading, discuss these questions:
—How is Ecclesiastes' treatment of death different from that in The Song of Solomon?
—Is it necessary to choose between the points of view expressed in Ecclesiastes and in The Song of Solomon, or can you see ways in which they can fit together? If so, how can this be done?
—Is it possible that the speaker in Psalm 73 is talking about the kind of love of God that is stronger than death? Why, or why not?

(F) Explore the points of the metaphors in The Song of Solomon.

Advance Preparation

Be sure to read ahead of time the "Additional Bible Helps" found at the end of this chapter. Also read the following words of explanation.

Flower names like "rose of Sharon" and "lily of the valley" or animal names like "gazelle" are little more than educated guesses for the translators of these ancient biblical texts. Translators have tried to use flower, plant, and animal names that English readers will recognize, but we really do not know what most of them looked like or smelled like.

Nevertheless, if a flower or fruit or animal name is used in a metaphor, it is important to try to determine the point of the comparison. It has been said that a metaphor is like a finger pointing at the moon. The trick in understanding a metaphor is to look in the direction in which the finger points and not at the finger itself.

Plant metaphors may be concerned with visual beauty, fragrance, color, texture, usual location (such as in wilderness areas, or on mountaintops), or the way in which the plant is used. For instance, when the woman refers to herself in 2:1 she names two flowers that might be understood as common wildflowers in her geographical location. Thus she may be saying that she is not particularly beautiful or remarkable in her setting. But the man tells her in the next verse that she stands out from the other women like a large, spectacular bloom surrounded by cactus plants.

Animal metaphors may evoke mental pictures of the way an animal looks or acts, where it is usually found, or how people feel about it. We sometimes attribute endearing characteristics to some kinds of animals and feel repulsed by others, without reference to their usefulness or to their ability to endanger our lives.

Comparisons with artistic objects may direct our attention toward visual similarities or toward the feelings that these objects evoke in the observer, or the point may have to do with the worth or value of the object.

- Divide class members into four groups.

Group 1
- Give Group 1 a large sheet of paper. Ask the group members to divide it into three sections. They are to label one part "human," the second part "nonhuman" and the third part "point."
- Ask group members to look at the metaphor in 5:13. Read the verse; then discuss:
—What is compared to what in the first two lines of the verse? What is the point of the comparison?
—What is compared with what in the last two lines of 5:13? What is the point of the comparison?
- The group then needs to fill in the chart at the appropriate sections, with *cheeks* under the column marked "human," and so forth.
- Ask Group 1 to appoint a spokesperson to report back to the whole group, sharing the group's conclusions and reasoning processes.

Group 2
- Ask this group to work with the verses in 4:1-5.
- Ask the group to discuss what the metaphors in its verses point to. If it is a sensory experience, which of the five senses (sight, sound, smell, touch, taste) are involved? If it is an emotional experience, what kind of emotion is evoked?
- Then ask the group to paraphrase the sense of the verse, stating in the group's own words what the man is trying to say about the woman's appearance.
- If people have difficulty understanding the metaphor in 4:4, ask such questions as:
—If this comparison were based on visual similarities, what image would you get of the woman's neck?
—If this metaphor were based on similarities of feelings evoked by the observation of the two things that are compared, what would be the point of the comparison?
—What kind of jewelry or ornamentation does this verse imply the woman was wearing?
- Ask a spokesperson from Group 2 to report to the whole group, sharing the group's conclusions and reasoning processes.

Group 3
- Give the following verses to Group 3 to analyze: 2:3; 2:8-9; 2:16-17; 4:13-14; 8:8-9.
- Ask this group to discuss what the metaphor in these verses points to.
- Ask a spokesperson from Group 3 to report back to the whole group, sharing the group's conclusions and reasoning processes.

Group 4
- Ask Group 4 to read 1:6; 5:1; 6:2; and 8:11-12 and answer this question:
—What do the terms *vineyard* and *garden* refer to?
- Group 4 should also appoint a spokesperson to report back to the whole group, sharing the group's conclusions and reasoning processes.

(G) "Analyze" the dream.

It has been suggested that 5:2-7 is a "dream sequence" in which the woman tells some of her friends (the "daughters of Jerusalem" in verse 8) about a dream that she had.

- Ask class members to read 5:2-7 silently. Then discuss these questions as a total group:
—Does 5:2-7 have elements in it that seem to be typical of dreams or not?
—If so, what do you think such a dream means or implies?

Dimension 3: What Does the Bible Mean to Us?

(H) Consider the power of love.

Part One
- Divide class members into pairs or groups of three to discuss some of the following questions:
—What does it mean to say that "love is strong as death?"
—Does this statement mean to imply that love will keep you alive? Can love keep someone from dying?
—What can love do over against the power of death?
—In what ways can love be fearsome ("cruel" or "fierce" or "relentless")? Is this a good thing or a bad thing to say about love?
—Have you experienced this kind of love in your life (either love that is stronger than death or fierce as the grave)?

Part Two
- Then ask the small groups to read 1 John 4:7-16. Discuss:
—What, if any, is the relationship between the love mentioned in The Song of Solomon and the love talked about in First John?

Part Three
- Call the class members back together. Ask these questions:
—Can you see how The Song of Solomon can be read both as poetry about human love and as a theological metaphor?
—If we understand The Song of Solomon to be an extended metaphor about God's love, then what does 8:6-7 say to us?
- Close by reading the following phrases from today's study: "God is love and those who abide in love abide in God...." "Love is strong as death.... Many waters cannot quench love, / neither can floods drown it."

(I) Explore issues of sexuality and the Bible.

The Song of Solomon is at one and the same time a picture of love between a man and a woman and a metaphor of God's love for us. In order to fully appreciate the theological metaphor we have to read and appreciate it first as love poetry. The "Additional Bible Helps" on page 67 in this leader's guide gives information on the history of interpretation for The Song of Solomon, which will help you with this Learning Option.

- Depending on the degree of comfort or openness you think your class members will feel, you might discuss some of the following issues in the whole group and others in pairs or in small groups.
- Read over the questions and decide what class configuration and which questions are best for your class:

Part One
- Read Genesis 1:27-31 and Genesis 2:21-25 aloud in class.
—What do these Genesis texts say about God's intentions regarding human sexuality? (Be sure to note God's evaluation of creation as "very good" in Genesis 1:31.)
—Do you think most people have a hard time believing that their bodies are "very good"? What makes you think so?
—Where do we get most of our attitudes or feelings about whether our bodies are good or not?
—What kinds of limitations do you think ought to be put on the expression of human sexuality?
—Does The Song of Solomon go beyond the bounds of what you find acceptable for the expression of human sexuality? If so, in what ways?
—How do societies or cultures differ in what they consider "acceptable" expressions of sexuality?
—How is the sexual attraction portrayed in The Song of Solomon like and how is it unlike what you usually see on television or in the movies?
—What conclusions have you drawn about the expression of human sexuality from your reading of The Song of Solomon?

Part Two
- Be sure to end your discussion of human sexuality in The Song of Solomon by spending some time on the theological connections that our traditions have made between God's love for humanity and human love. If you have not yet done so, look carefully at Song of Solomon 8:6-7. Then discuss as a whole class or in small groups the following question:
—If we understand The Song of Solomon to be an extended metaphor about God's love, then what does 8:6-7 say to us?
- Close by reading 1 John 4:7-16 aloud to the group.

(J) Wrap up your study of the Wisdom Literature.

- Ask people to read or review the article on "Wisdom Literature" in the study book, page 3.
- On the chalkboard or on large sheets of paper, list the books of Job, Proverbs, Ecclesiastes, and The Song of Solomon.
- Consider each book, asking the following questions for each book and jotting down the class's consensus:
—What was the primary theological (God-related) problem considered or confronted in this book?
—What did the author or authors of this book want us to learn from their writings?
—What did the author or authors of this book think it was important for people to do?
—What (if anything) does The Song of Solomon have in common with the other wisdom writings?
- In conclusion, ask people to answer these questions:
—What new learnings or insights have you gained from the study of the wisdom writings and Psalms?

—What parts of these biblical books have seemed particularly relevant to where you are right now in your faith journey?
—What new questions have been raised in your mind by the materials you have read from this section of the Bible?
• In closing, ask those class members who feel comfortable to share favorite verses from the Scriptures studied.

Additional Bible Helps

History of Interpetation
An early Jewish commentator concluded that "the Song of Solomon resembles locks to which the keys have been lost."

Early Jewish and Christian interpreters insisted that The Song of Solomon was primarily a book about God and not a book about humankind. Up until the middle of the nineteenth century, most Jewish readers understood The Song of Solomon as an allegory about God's love for Israel and most Christian readers understood it as an allegory about Christ's love for the church.

Modern readers are mostly inclined to let the poetry of The Song of Solomon speak for itself. This does not mean, however, that modern readers think The Song of Solomon is purely secular or nonreligious. Old Testament texts clearly say that the physical attraction between the sexes was created by God and that God considered this creation to be "very good."

Nevertheless, modern people may have difficulty reading and discussing the meaning of The Song of Solomon. People in our culture often have a hard time believing that the pleasure they can receive from their bodies is good in God's eyes. Although the parts of the human body all possess names in English, the degree to which any of these names may be used in public or in polite company varies from culture to culture and from generation to generation within the same culture. In England during the time of Queen Victoria, it was considered vulgar to use the word *leg* even to refer to the leg of a table, and in some circles in modern America, people use *white meat* to refer to the breast of a chicken.

However, quite a bit of evidence indicates that it was customary to sing songs in praise of the bride or groom at weddings in ancient Israel (see Jeremiah 33:10-11). And a number of Egyptian, Mesopotamian, and Canaanite love songs describing the various parts of the male or female body have been discovered in recent decades, indicating that Near Eastern cultures may have been less reticent than we often are in such matters. The singing of songs describing the beauty of the newly married couple was a custom that persisted up until relatively recent times in Palestinian and Syrian rural communities.

The presence of The Song of Solomon in the Bible reminds us that the love of a human couple for each other originates with God. The Song of Solomon speaks of a loving bond that includes both sexual attraction and the kind of love that is able to survive even the death of the loved one.

Translation Problems
The metaphors that are used for the praise of physical beauty in any language are closely bound to the culture from which they come. A common endearment in one language may sound ridiculous or even insulting when translated literally into another language and culture (for example, it is acceptable to call your loved one "my little cabbage" in French [*mon petit chouchou*], but not in English). Even within the same culture and the same language, common metaphors change over time. Thus, attempts to translate the ancient Near Eastern poetry of The Song of Solomon into English often result in comparisons that sound strange or silly to our modern Western ears.

The names of plants and animals are used both in setting the background scene for the poetry and in the metaphors describing the parts of the beloved's body. Most of these names are difficult, if not impossible to translate with any degree of precision. For instance, the Hebrew of The Song of Solomon may use a word that is translated "apple," but the translators know that the fruit we call an apple was not grown in ancient Israel. Even if we could identify the plant or animal named, we might not recognize the images or the feelings that were evoked by naming these things. Such words have associations that are are often culture-bound. Thus, for instance, roses are associated in our own culture with positive loving emotions (in spite of the fact that they have thorns on their stems). When we say someone has *apples* in her or his cheeks, we think of an attractive, healthy shade of red, even though we know that there are such things as green and yellow apples. The same is true with metaphors drawn from the animal world. It may be considered complimentary to call someone a *kitten*, but it is insulting to call the same person a *cat*.

Another cultural assumption that affects the translation of The Song of Solomon has to do with the perception of beauty. In older English versions (such as King James, Revised Standard, and New International versions) translators assumed that the woman who speaks in 1:5 claims that she is attractive *in spite of* her dark skin. Thus they translate "I am black/dark *but/yet* beautiful/ lovely/comely." However, in Hebrew, there is no separate word that means what an English speaker means by the word *but*. The word that is usually translated "and" serves both purposes. Translators make the choice to translate the Hebrew word one way or the other, depending on their reading of the meaning of the Hebrew sentence. Cultural biases led some translators to assume that darkness of skin was detrimental to beauty. But the New Revised Standard Version goes back to the literal sense of the Hebrew with its translation: "I am black *and* beautiful" (italics added).

A Closer Look at the Psalms

By Kathleen Farmer

The name *Psalms* comes from the Greek word *psalmoi* (sahm-OI), which refers to songs sung to the accompaniment of stringed instruments. The term *Psalter* (which is sometimes used as another name for the Book of Psalms) originally referred to an ancient musical instrument resembling a zither. The Hebrew name for the whole collection of 150 biblical psalms is *tehillim* (tuh-HIL-im), which means "praises."

The Book of Psalms is usually divided into five shorter collections (also called "books"). Each of the first four "books" ends with a short doxology (a hymn of praise to God).

Book 1 = Psalms 1–41
Doxology =
"Blessed be the LORD, the God of Israel,
from everlasting to everlasting.
Amen and Amen."
(Psalm 41:13)

Book 2 = Psalms 42–72
Doxology =
"Blessed be the LORD, the God of Israel,
who alone does wondrous things.
Blessed be his glorious name forever;
may his glory fill the whole earth.
Amen and Amen."
(Psalm 72:18-19)

Book 3 = Psalms 73–89
Doxology =
"Blessed be the LORD forever.
Amen and Amen."
(Psalm 89:52)

Book 4 = Psalms 90–106
Doxology =
"Blessed be the LORD, the God of Israel,
from everlasting to everlasting.
And let all the people say,
'Amen.'
Praise the LORD!"
(Psalm 106:48)

Book 5 = Psalms 107–150
Psalm 150 acts as a concluding doxology for both the fifth "book" and for the whole Book of Psalms.

Titles or Headings
All but thirty-four of the psalms have titles or headings. The psalm headings were probably written later than the psalms themselves. However, the headings were already in place when the Hebrew Bible was translated into Greek (two or three centuries before the time of Jesus). A psalm heading may say something about the people or groups of people with whom the psalm was associated (Moses, Psalm 90; Sons of Korah, Psalm 42). Some of the psalms linked with David's name also say something about particular historical circumstances (such as Psalms 18 or 63). Other headings refer to particular types of psalms (Psalms 16; 17), to musical settings for the performance of a psalm (Psalm 22), to musical instruments used in accompanying the psalm (Psalms 4; 6; 54), or to directions for the use of the psalm in worship settings (as in Psalms 38 or 100).

The meanings of many of the technical (musical and liturgical) terms used in the psalm headings have been lost. *Mizmor* (miz-MORE, which is used fifty-seven times) is usually translated "psalm" (meaning "a song with accompaniment"). The term *maskil* (MAS-kil, which occurs fifteen times, mostly in Books 2 and 3) probably means a "clever" psalm in which a certain kind of name-play is used (such as a pun on the name of the person to whom or about whom it is sung).

The phrase "According to . . ." followed by such things as "Do Not Destroy" (Psalms 57; 58; 59; 75), "The Deer of the Dawn" (Psalm 22), or "Lillies" (45; 49) probably refers to the melody of a popular song to which the psalm was to be sung.

Names for God in the Psalms

When the psalmists pray they usually address their prayers either to the Lord or to God. The English translation *God* represents various forms of the Hebrew words *El* (el) and *Elohim* (EL-oh-him). The English term *Lord* (when presented as LORD, in capital and small capital letters) represents various forms of the Hebrew word *Yahweh* (YAH-weh), which was considered to be the God of Israel's personal name.

In some ways these two divine names are interchangeable. However, the word *Lord* (LORD) is used about twice as often in the Psalter as the word *God* (some 800 uses of LORD compared to about 400 for God). An exact count is difficult because different manuscripts vary slightly. The distribution of the names used for the Deity varies considerably among the five sections or "books" of the Psalms. In Book 1 (Psalms 1–41), *Lord* occurs around 280 times while *God* appears only 65 times. But the psalmists who speak in Books 2 and 3 prefer to address their prayers to *God* (using the Hebrew word *Elohim* and its variants) rather than to the *Lord* (using the Hebrew word *Yahweh*). *God* occurs about 165 times and *Lord* (as LORD meaning Yahweh) appears only 27 times in Book 2. However, in Book 4 (Psalms 90–106), *Lord* (LORD) is used over a hundred times and *God* is used only 28 times.

This difference in usage of divine names may have originated because of regional dialects. The psalmists who preferred the name Elohim (God) may have come from the Northern Kingdom of Israel. Refugees who fled south to Judah and Jerusalem when the Northern Kingdom fell to the Assyrians may have brought their own favorite psalms with them. At a later time the northern psalms using Elohim (God) may have been combined with Judean psalms using Yahweh (LORD), resulting in the present form of the Book of Psalms.

Pre-Canonical Collections

The headings and the names used for God in the various psalms indicate that several smaller groupings of psalms existed originally as independent collections before they were incorporated into the final canonical version of the Psalter. There are at least two groups of Psalms associated with David. The first Davidic collection (Psalms 3–41) uses the name *Yahweh* (LORD) far more often than the name *Elohim* (God).

The second Davidic collection (Psalms 51–70, with the exception of 66 and 67) has a distinctly Elohistic (EL-oh-hist-ik) inclination. This can be seen by comparing Psalm 53 with Psalm 14. Psalms 14 and 53 are very similar, except for the names they use for God. Psalm 53 seems to be an Elohistic reworking of Psalm 14. In Psalm 53, the divine name is changed from Yahweh to Elohim in three out of four references.

Songs by and for Pilgrims

Psalms 120–134 all begin with the phrase "A Song of Ascents," but it is not clear what these psalms have in common, other than their titles. The term *ascents* may refer to the last stage in the climb up the hill to Jerusalem or up the steps of the Temple complex. Prophetic texts often speak of going "up" to Zion (Jeremiah 31:6) or "up to the mountain of the LORD" (Micah 4:2). Thus these Psalms of Ascent may once have been a collection of inspirational songs used by pilgrims on their way to worship in the Temple in Jerusalem.

The Psalms of Asaph

There are a total of twelve Psalms in the Psalter that mention the name Asaph (AY-saf) in their headings. The first Psalm of Asaph is found in Book 2 (Psalm 50) and the other eleven Psalms of Asaph are found in Book 3 (Psalms 73–83). According to 1 Chronicles 6:33-47, Asaph was a Levite. In 1 Chronicles 15:17-19, 16:4-5, Asaph is described as a Levite musician who played a leading role during David's time. Ezra 3:10 indicates Asaph's descendants carried on their ancestor's musical functions, and Ezra 2:41 (Nehemiah 7:44) names the Asaphites as the only levitical singers who returned from the Babylonian Exile.

The Psalms of the Sons of Korah

Eleven psalms mention the "sons of Korah (KOR-uh)" in their headings: 42–49 (with the exception of 43) and 84–88 (with the exception of 86). Although Psalm 43 does not have a heading, it is similar in many ways to Psalm 42 and may once have been considered the twelfth psalm of the sons of Korah. In the historical narratives, Korah is said to be one of the descendants of Levi, through Levi's son Kohath (Exodus 6:16-24). According to Numbers 16, Korah was one of the leaders of a rebellion against Moses and Aaron in the period of the wilderness wanderings. Korah seems to have perished as a consequence of his attempt to seek priestly equality with the descendants of Aaron (Numbers 16:31-35), but the "sons of Korah" apparently survived (Numbers 26:11). The Chronicler describes the singing of the sons of Korah as a crucial element in leading the armies of Israel to victory in a much later period (2 Chronicles 20:18-22). Heman (who is mentioned in the heading of Psalm 88) is also said to be a son of Korah in 1 Chronicles 6:33-37.

Thus it seems that there may once have been earlier collections that were known as the "Korahite" psalms or the "Asaphite" psalms. The different guilds of temple singers may once have included the psalms that bear their names in their repertoire, or these psalms may have some other qualities that set them apart. But now these earlier collections have been incorporated into the final form of the Psalter.

Poetic Structures

The basic poetic unit (consisting of parallel thoughts) can be seen even in English translations of the Psalms, as can the poetic use of repeated lines and phrases. Repetitions that occur on a regular basis (as in Psalm 136) are easy to spot. A more subtle form of repetition called an "inclusion" or "an envelope structure" uses the same set of words to mark the beginning and the end of the psalm (as in Psalms 8 and 103). Other poetic devices used in Hebrew poetry are more difficult to spot. At least nine psalms (Psalms 9–10; 25; 34; 37; 11; 112; 119; 145) can be called "acrostic (uh-KROS-tik) psalms." Each of these psalms is structured around an alphabetic acrostic pattern in which half-lines, verses, or even whole stanzas begin with a different Hebrew letter, in alphabetic order.

Knowing that a psalm has been written according to an acrostic pattern helps explain some things about the content of these psalms. For instance, Psalm 25 has only twenty-two verses, just as the Hebrew alphabet has twenty-two letters. The choppiness (or somewhat disconnected nature) of the psalm's train of thought is explained by the speaker's desire to start each subsequent verse with the right Hebrew letter.

Psalm 119 is unusually long (176 verses) because each of the twenty-two letters of the alphabet is used eight times. Thus the first eight verses of the psalm begin with the first letter of the alphabet, the second set of eight (verses 9-16) all begin with the second letter of the alphabet, and so on until the end.

Psalms 9 and 10, taken together, make up an almost complete acrostic, but the pattern is irregular. Although the Hebrew Bible lists these psalms as two separate units, in the earliest Greek Bibles the two together were counted as one psalm.

Popular Theology in Wisdom Literature and Psalms

By Kathleen Farmer

If you ask an average group of Christians what they think heaven will be like, you will probably get as many different answers as there are people in the group. Even in "confessional" churches (churches that have doctrinal standards that members have to agree to believe) many beliefs are assumed rather than stated. "Popular theology" (what ordinary people think and believe about God, about the world and their place in it) has always co-existed alongside "official" religious doctrines.

In Israel, there were no "official" doctrines that people had to believe in order to be considered faithful worshipers of God. But there were many things that people took for granted. Judging from what biblical speakers say, it seems that most Israelites expected God to reward the faithful and punish the wicked in this life (not after death).

The Concept of Sheol

Sheol (SHEE-ohl) was the name Israelites often used to refer to the place where everyone (the good and the bad alike) ended up after death. *Sheol* seems to have been considered a shadowy kind of underworld, an abode of the dead (Proverbs 9:18). In some places, *Sheol* is used as a synonym for death or the state of being dead. *Sheol* is sometimes equated with the grave (as in Psalm 49:14) or with another undefined place called "the Pit" (Psalm 16:10). And on at least one occasion, *Sheol* is personified, as if it had some active mythological existence in its own right (Isaiah 5:14).

However, just as Christians differ widely in the ways they picture heaven, different Israelites pictured Sheol and what happened to the dead after death in different ways. Isaiah 14:9-20 implies that the dead have some memory of who they were in their lives under the sun. But Ecclesiastes says "the dead know nothing" (Ecclesiastes 9:5) and "their love and their hate and their envy have already perished" as soon as they die (9:6).

Sometimes the realm of the dead is thought to be a place of silence and rest, where everything related to human joys and concerns disappears (Job 3:11-19). According to Job, "those who go down to Sheol" are like a cloud that "fades and vanishes" (Job 7:9). And Psalm 88:12 speaks of death as "the land of forgetfulness."

Some of the psalmists think the dead are unable to remember God or to praise the Lord (Psalms 6:5; 30:9; 88:10). Other psalmists think that the dead are "cut off" from God and are no longer remembered by the Lord (Psalm 88:5). But the speaker in Psalm 139 disagrees, saying to the Lord, "if I make my bed in Sheol, you are there" (139:8).

The speaker in Psalm 88 does not expect the Lord to "work wonders for the dead" (Psalm 88:10). But the speaker in Psalm 73 expects God to "receive" the faithful with honor after death (73:24).

One thing no Old Testament witness ever says about Sheol: no one ever says that Sheol will be a place of punishment for the wicked after death. The popular modern picture of the punishing fires of "Hell" was never a part of either popular or official theology in Israel.

The Concept of "Soul"
In the Psalms, God is sometimes said to save or to "deliver" the psalmist's "soul" from Sheol (as in Psalms 30:3 or 86:13). In modern popular theology, the soul is sometimes thought to be separate from the body—an immortal spark or essence of life that lives on after a person's body dies. But in Old Testament texts, the word *nephesh* (NEH-fesh, which is translated "soul" in many contexts) has a much wider range of meaning than the modern idea of "soul." This can be seen by looking at the variety of ways in which the word *nephesh* has been used in Old Testament texts.

In Genesis 1:20, 24, 30, and 2:7 the word *nephesh* refers to a living being, either human or animal. If *nephesh* were translated as "soul," Genesis 1:20 would read "And God said, 'Let the waters bring forth swarms of living souls.'"

In Exodus 21:23, Deuteronomy 12:23-24, and Judges 12:3 the word *nephesh* is translated in most English Bibles by the word "life." If the word *nephesh* were translated "soul" in Exodus 21, then the law of equivalent restitution for damages ("an eye for an eye and a tooth for a tooth") would allow the taking of a "soul" for a "soul" (Exodus 21:23).

In many other places, the word *nephesh* is simply a synonym for "person" as in Genesis 46:18 (Zilpah gave birth to sixteen "souls") or Exodus 1:5 ("The total number of people [souls] born to Jacob was seventy"). In Old Testament usage, "soul" can refer either to a living person or to a dead person. In Numbers 6:6 the term "dead *nephesh*" is translated in the NRSV as "corpse."

The most frequent way in which *nephesh* is used is as a synonym for one's self. People commonly used the phrase "my *nephesh*" (or your *nephesh*, his or her *nephesh*, and so on) to mean my*self* or me (or your*self* or you, and so on). This usage can be seen in Psalm 7:2, "like a lion they will tear *me* [literally my *nephesh*] apart."

Thus it can be seen from the texts themselves that one does not *have* a "soul," but one *is* a "soul" in the popular thinking of Old Testament authors. Modern popular ideas about the "soul" as an entity that exists apart from the body originated in the writings of Greek philosophers of religion.

Recommended Further Reading

The Book of Job, translated and with an introduction by Stephen Mitchell (North Point Press, 1987); ISBN 0-86547-270-X. Out of print; may be available in libraries. Formerly published as *Into the Whirlwind* (Doubleday, 1979).

The Book of Psalms; Volume 6 of Message of Biblical Spirituality Series, by Toni Craven (The Liturgical Press, 1992); ISBN 0-8146-5572-6.

Love Lyrics From the Bible: A Translation and Literary Study of the Song of Songs; volume 4 of Bible and Literature Series; by Marcia Falk (The Almond Press [England], 1982); ISBN 0-907459-07-2. Out of print; may be available in libraries.

The Message of the Psalms, by Walter Brueggemann (Augsburg Publishing House, 1984); ISBN 0-8066-2120-6, 10-4370.

Proverbs and Ecclesiastes: Who Knows What Is Good? International Theological Commentary Series, by Kathleen A. Farmer, edited by Frederick C. Holmgren and George A. Knight (Eerdmans, 1991); ISBN 0-8028-0161-7.

When Bad Things Happen to Good People; by Harold S. Kushner (Schocken Books, 1981); ISBN 0-8052-4089-6.

Wisdom Literature; Volume 5 of Message of Biblical Spirituality Series, by Kathleen M. O'Connor (The Liturgical Press, 1988); ISBN 0-8146-5571-8.

PROVERBS
Sampling the Shorter Sayings

On Advice
11:14; 12:15; 13:10; 15:22; 19:20; 20:18; 24:6

On Anger and Arguments
14:17, 29; 15:1, 18; 17:14; 19:11, 19; 20:3; 26:17, 20-21; 29:8, 11, 22

On Business Dealings
11:1, 26; 16:11; 20:10, 14, 23

On the Fear of the LORD
10:27; 14:26-27; 15:16, 33; 16:6; 19:23; 22:4

On Gossip or Slander
10:18; 11:12-13; 16:28; 18:8; 26:22

On Humility
11:2; 15:33; 18:12; 22:4; 27:2; 29:23

On Hypocrisy
12:9; 18:24; 20:5-6; 25:14; 26:23-25; 27:5-6

On Justice
17:15, 23, 26; 18:5, 17, 18; 19:5, 9, 28; 21:15; 22:8

On Laziness
10:26; 12:24; 13:4; 19:24; 20:13; 22:13; 26:13-16

On Poverty and Wealth
10:4; 11:4, 28; 13:23; 14:20-21;
15:16-17; 16:8, 19; 17:1; 18:11; 28:6, 8, 11, 19, 20, 22

On Pride
11:2; 13:10; 15:25; 16:5, 18; 18:12; 21:4

On Truth and Lies
10:18; 12:17, 19, 22; 14:5, 25; 20:17; 21:6, 28

On Uses and Misuses of Speech
10:18-19; 11:9, 11; 12:13-14, 18; 13:3;
14:3; 15:1-2, 4, 23; 16:23; 17:27-28; 18:6-8, 20-21; 20:19; 21:23; 26:22

Sample Psalm–Line

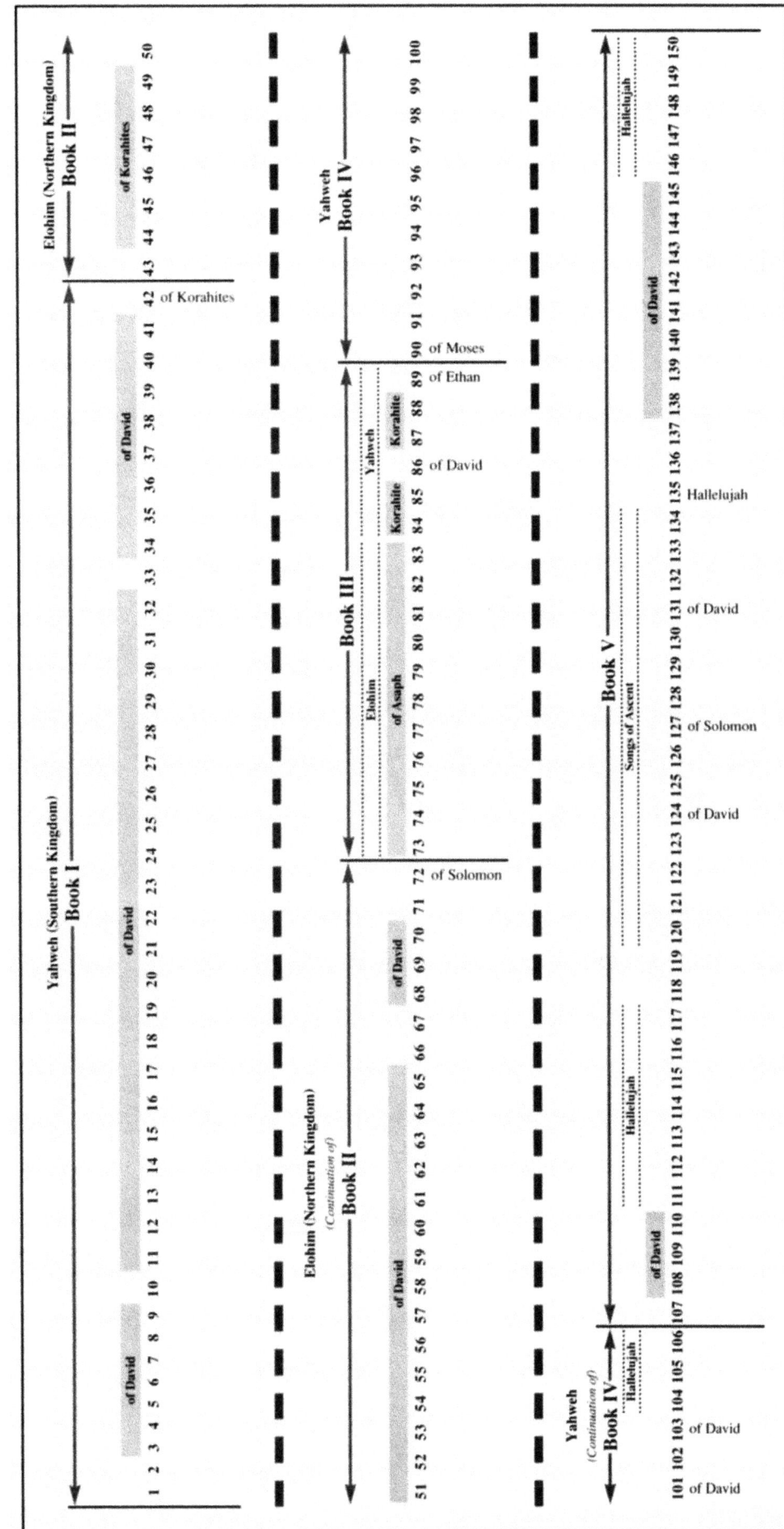

Information included in this chart:
Biblical authorship notations (NRSV)
"Names for God" (see page 69)
Use of Hallelujah (see page 22)

Adapted from the work of Len Wilson, minister of electronic media

www.ingramcontent.com/pod-product-compliance
Lightning Source LLC
LaVergne TN
LVHW061315060426
835507LV00019B/2172